adrian paci
the guardians

AF622958

edited by / a cura di
gabi scardi

mousse publishing

chiostri di sant'eustorgio
kaufmann repetto
galerie peter kilchmann

present, elsewhere, beyond

by gabi scardi

Adrian Paci makes art, work after work, through an ongoing, never definitive engagement with the present time and context, with art history and the artistic act itself. His practice draws on a deep familiarity with the art of the past, combining the observation of social dynamics in our time with an awareness of how actions endure through different places and times and thereby take on iconic depth and significance; it explores the layered meanings and interpretative possibilities of signs and images.

As a space of thought and knowledge for the expression and transmission of meaning, each work is grounded not only in an imaginative sensibility, but in a capacity to pick up signals from within and without. Paci moves with a clarity of mind and keenness of vision that reflect an ethical attitude. His relationship with reality is based on tension, attention, and precision; on receptiveness and commitment; but also on individuality and distance; which are both a need and a liberation.

Key motifs in his works include travel, passage, waiting—which is above all a state of expectation—and ties to one's time and place of origin, which are not dimensions to which anyone can return, but rather deep touchstones that individuals must carry with them. These themes are examined in an active relationship with knowledge, seen as the filter through which we decipher the world.

Albanian by birth and Italian by choice since 1997, Adrian Paci grew up under the regime of Enver Hoxha, which sealed off the country and proclaimed the dawn of a new humanity, the perfect outgrowth of nationalistic communist ideology. In the 1990s, as his nation sank into chaos, Paci moved to Italy, discovering all the contradictions of a different society that also seemed bent on generating a new version of mankind: the consumption-based, individualistic, standardized and increasingly globalized West we all know. That may be why he isn't prone to sweeping statements or swayed by fashions, and remains wary of abstract, universal positions. But nor is he satisfied with contingencies. He is drawn to actions and expressions that may be commonplace, yet contain both solemnity and restraint, whose deep and ancient roots give them the quality of archetypes. They move beyond the limits of space and time, tangibly showing the cultural substrate that links human beings together like a common denominator. These are acts, gestures, and attitudes such as a handshake, the subject of *The Encounter* (2011); the tense expression of a bride saying goodbye to the family she is leaving to be wed, in *The Kiss* (2008); the intent faces of the men in *The Column* (2013) who are quarrying a huge block of marble from the mountain; or the weathered ones of those waiting to journey towards a more decent life in *The Line* (2007), or at least find a job for the day in *Turn On* (2004).

Significantly, *The Guardians* opens with the photographic sequence *The Encounter*: It shows the parvis of an ancient church; at the center stands a man shaking hands with hundreds of people who come up to him, dressed in their weekday clothes. They converge for reasons and from places unknown, then move on, leaving him there. A handshake is simple, ordinary, concrete, yet meaningful: it is a greeting, an exchange, a pact, a bond. In *The Encounter*, its ritual aspect is accentuated both by the fact that it occurs in a space of respect, a buffer zone between the place of worship and the public street, and by its repetition, which turns it into a sort of ceremony. Life is given its authentic substance by how we interact with others on an everyday basis; and this encounter in and of itself is a ceremony worthy of celebration.

Paci's interest in these eloquent actions does not cut him off from current events; rather, he places the latter against the backdrop of a long, deep past, to help us grasp their more specific and urgent dynamics. His investigation hinges on the relationship between politics, economics, and social justice, the contemporary crisis in the concept of citizenship, and specifically, the status of those who are forced to leave their homes; on emigration, exile, uprooting. He is engrossed by the state of separation and limbo in which fugitives and refugees must live, and their search for asylum. The figure of the migrant is close to Paci's heart. This can clearly be seen in *The Line* and in the two videos *Klodi* (2005) and *My Song in Your Kitchen* (2017).

The first is a photographic diptych showing a queue of people on a deserted runway; individuals full of potential, but blocked, isolated, waiting in silence for a plane that isn't there. Different levels of reflection intersect in this work: a more universal one of human life as eternal transit—it is the sense of precariousness, the idea of an "elsewhere" that is always with us, the unpredictable journey of existence—and another connected to the phenomenon of migration, the many people now forced to set out on journeys of hope towards other countries; countries that in many cases prove inhospitable and trap them in a painful or even tragic limbo. Despite its seeming simplicity, this image, like the entire series of connected works (including the iconic *Centro di permanenza temporanea,* 2007), presents itself with an urgency and poetic scope that can engender profound experiences of connection and resonance.

Klodi is the live video portrait of a young man eternally in transit, eternally in search of a better future, in search of work, of rights, of an easier life, or simply some way to get by. But in a world where identity is defined and controlled by national politics, he is not allowed to reinvent himself, or forge new social ties. Klodi epitomizes the uprooted individual: cut off from places and people, hidden and vulnerable, constantly on the run; in the spiral progression of history, the idea of "making a home" for himself is increasingly impossible to achieve. And he ends up in a dramatic, absurd state of constant peregrination, whose outcome is unknown. Paci takes the time to hear his tale. As we listen to his voice, the routes along which he has traveled through Europe appear on the screen, traced by hand: the alternative geography of a person forced into a precarious, stateless existence. But what lingers is his story, unshackled from silence, and the expression on his face—troubled but full of life, rescued from invisibility and seen for once in close-up.

My Song in Your Kitchen, on the other hand, is a video shot at Casa Monluè in Milan: a center temporarily housing refugees who have been granted asylum. These are spaces humming with humanity, brimming with nostalgia, and straining towards the future. Here Paci has established a link between food and music, which are both tied to the emotional sphere and childhood memories, to our closest, most basic relationships, to everyday customs in the places we come from; vibrant dimensions infused with stories and memories, which both channel longings and convey a sense of conviviality. At the artist's invitation, the uninviting, impersonal kitchens at the shelter are used to prepare a shared meal, while singing, and become spaces of interaction. In the actions of the young participants, who come from different countries around Africa—in the simple foods, the hands carrying out familiar tasks, the sounds they have brought with them from home—we can glimpse fragments of their past lives. Paci has also interwoven the images with an Albanian song, played by an Italian group. This bridges the distance from them, creating a profound, often joyous sense of shared experience. The video opens and closes with long, empty hallways lined with closed doors on either side, which continue to convey a feeling of transition and of the unknown.

It is no accident that this work, made in a place that is marginalized in every sense— socially, geographically, mentally—was placed in the magnificent space of Sant'Eustorgio: rather, it is an invitation to reflect on the lonely, desperate state of people who have just come to a new country, and also on their potential, their desire to work together and take pleasure in contributing something, and on everyone's right to exist.

A sense of intimacy can be found in all of Adrian Paci's work. It is an intimacy that is not about withdrawing from the world, but rather, focusing one's gaze; that does not shrink the sphere of experience, but rather deepens it. In *The Future of Nostalgia*,[1] Svetlana Boym calls this "diasporic intimacy" and sees it as a special form of bonding that has a foothold in personal experience; "Diasporic intimacy," writes Boym, "could be seen as the mutual attraction of two immigrants from different parts of the world or the sense of a precarious coziness of a

1 Svetlana Boym, *The Future of Nostalgia* (New York: Basic Books, 2001).

foreign home. Just as one learns to live with alienation and reconciles oneself to the uncanniness of the surrounding world and to the strangeness of the human touch, there comes a surprise, a pang of intimate recognition, a hope that sneaks in through the back door in the mist of the habitual estrangement of everyday life abroad."

In Paci's work, this form of identification that springs from the overlap between individual and shared experience moves far beyond the personal sphere, raising questions of an ethical, aesthetic, and political nature. What is more: exploring the intersection between these different planes, Paci sees the migrant state as describing not only the entire history of man, but the natural condition of the artist, a constant incitement to imagine new ways of living, new possible relationships with our surroundings, new languages of expression.

A prime example of his skill for forging links between the personal stories and shared memories, turning the individual body into a collective archetype, is *Home to Go*: a sculpture in which the artist portrays himself life size, stripped of everything, walking along with the roof of a house on his back. This piece was made in 2001; in the same period, Paci developed an entire body of work around the theme of separation and loss that included *Back Home* (2001) and *Vajtojca* (2002). But here his symbolism reaches its greatest incisiveness and intensity.

Alone in a spotlight at the center of Sant'Eustorgio's vast sacristy, the figure stands as both witness and monument, eloquently expressing the struggle to move forward while encumbered by the past, and by the heavy burden of a many-layered identity. Reconciling one's sense of belonging with the reality of displacement is a complex and wrenching experience. Life itself seems to become a strain and trial. But by moving beyond grief, the work seems to say, one can resume the journey.

Home to Go centers on the man, the wayfarer, the pilgrim, and reminds viewers that we are all unique and important; and that we are all foreigners here, endlessly journeying across the world's stage. Moreover, the work resonates with its sanctified surroundings, with the liturgical objects and reliquaries, powerfully evoking a dimension above and beyond human actions. The upside-down roof resembles a pair of wings unfurled to welcome whatever may arrive.

While all of Paci's work is infused with a primal spirituality and touches on something beyond the ephemeral, worldly realm, *Home to Go* makes an obvious reference to the religious iconography of the Passion. This is a theme that Paci returned to in many works over the course of a decade, such as *Cappella Pasolini* (2005) and *Via Crucis* (2011) for the church of San Bartolomeo in Milan. Since the artist grew up in a country that not only denied access to the outside world but to any experience outside the material realm, the idea of a religious and spiritual dimension was something he always connected with through the books of ancient art left to him by his father Ferdinand Paci, himself a painter: a legacy that was like a discovery, an experience, a means of training the eye.

This deeply assimilated knowledge of classical art emerges throughout his work in different ways. The various possibilities Paci explores have included recreating ancient images using modern techniques, and vice versa. A case in point is *Brothers* (2010). In the Portinari Chapel, this mosaic forges a dialogue with the Renaissance fresco cycle by Vincenzo Foppa and the arch by Giovanni di Balduccio depicting Saint Peter Martyr. *Brothers* is juxtaposed with the arch and lined up on the same visual axis, so that it can also be seen between its columns. Like other works in the "Passages" series, *Brothers* is based on a fragment of archival film, one of the many that the artist has collected: often amateur footage depicting traditional ceremonies or moments of everyday life, mostly in Albania. In this case the frame that has been chosen captures a fleeting interaction between two brothers; this tiny, completely marginal story has been reconstructed using an ancient, rigidly codified, almost obsolete technique; one that does not allow for much detail, and tends to freeze images into solemn fixity.

In *Brothers*, the technical characteristics and tactile quality of mosaic lend power to the image, giving it a sense of stability, as if stretched out over time. Nevertheless, amazingly, it retains the dynamic feel of the video, preserving the fleeting nature of a snapshot and the idea of moving light. This is achieved not in a traditional way through the shine of the tiles, but with irregularly chiseled heights and protrusions that generate the effect of light and shadow. The tessellated marble and enamel also evokes the pixels of the grainy video. The resulting image is an enigmatic one, where the simple gestures continue to convey intimacy, but also acquire intensity, monumentality, and a sense of the absolute. And so, through an analytical attention to detail and full awareness of the tools and language of art, Paci combines the contemplated, examined time of mosaic with the virtual quality of video, through the physicality of a technique reinvented from within.

The work grows out of both Paci's interest in the innumerable possibilities of interpretation contained in each image, and his conviction that in looking at the world around us, we tend even today to grasp the same visual structures that artists of the past used to construct their paintings. Masaccio, in particular, is called to mind by the figure of Rasha, whom we encounter in the video bearing her name (*Rasha*, 2017). Paci channels the Tuscan artist's spirit in the editing of this work.

Rasha Meish is a Palestinian woman who came from Syria to Rome in 2016 along a humanitarian corridor. The video shows her sharing her story, which she has asked to tell. But the images we see are the moments between sentences when the woman sits silently, waiting while her words are translated. Her physical presence is a powerful one. We see her listening to her own story, as her posture, her gestures, and the shifting expressions on her face convey not only the strain of the momentarily interrupted narrative, but the power of the experience she has lived through; an experience that despite all efforts to get its essence across, cannot be entirely summed up in words.

As the artist points out, between the verbal narrative and the bodily one, "between the silent face and the voice speaking Arabic, a gap emerges": Rasha becomes the protagonist not only of her story, but of the act of listening to it. Printed separately, on a sheet of paper that visitors are free to keep, are her translated words: necessary, but not enough. The work is a reflection on the traces left on our bodies by the past and how the body itself conveys them. The nuances of expression on the woman's face speak louder than words. *Rasha* is a work about the complexity of storytelling; about how an experience becomes a story and becomes language, not just through speech, but through the body. Her story is one of violence, of separation from places and people; it is a story of trauma, but also of the solace that can be found in fellowship and friendship. It must be heard, because through it one can sense the pain of countless other people. That is why, as in other works, Paci lingers on her face. Not for descriptive ends, but as an act of respect for the individual; for every individual. And so everything shifts from the plane of contingency to that of symbolism.

Within today's overcrowded visual universe, among a mountain of images, Rasha's face stands out, clear and vivid. And so, with one eye on these images, the other keeping watch on the world around him, and a restless imagination, Paci probes the work as it unfolds. This process acts as a filter and creates a distance that allows him, once again, to describe an era and its contradictions, turning an individual story into one that embodies an infinity of others.

In the Sala dell'Arciconfraternita where it is shown, *Rasha* becomes part of a choral narrative; the video is placed at the center of an eighteenth-century series of large-scale devotional paintings. The presentation evokes the narrative significance of the great painting cycles of the past, but also calls to mind a frame-based approach to film theory. Rasha's mutable, responsive expressions weave a dialogue with the dramatic, emphatic gestures of the painted characters, with the mechanical camera substituting the manual technique, and the typically cinematic fixed shot, horizontal and in extreme close up, replacing the animated, stage-like setting found in the paintings. This alternation of tools and methods reflects a shift in era. Yet however different, the figures are linked by the emotional force behind them, emphasized in both cases by the lighting.

Malgrado tutto (2017) also describes the unquenchable human need for expression. It is a series of photographs showing the graffiti that can still be seen on the peeling walls of the cells in an ancient Franciscan monastery that served as a prison during Enver Hoxha's communist dictatorship. From the end of World War II up to the 1990s, Albanian prisoners were shut away here, interrogated, and tortured. Partially restored to its original monastic function, and partially transformed into a Museum of Memory, the place still bears the traces of their silent suffering: drawings, words, calendars scratched into the walls to keep track of time. It is evidence—ephemeral, but still intense—of the human need to leave a trace of our passage, even in conditions of utter privation. The artist captures them in photographs before they disappear, in a commentary on his own country and its transformations that expands out to touch the great themes of time, memory, and forgetting.

Once again, the work involves a shift between different modes of expression. Paci's investigation deals with the different languages that constantly coexist and intersect in the world, and that can only be partially translated into each other. It is precisely by drawing on this linguistic complexity that the richness of everything around us can be expressed.

Malgrado tutto was presented on the walls of Sant'Eustorgio's early Christian cemetery. The fragile yet enduring signs of Albania's recent past are juxtaposed with the steles and epigraphs that have emerged from archeological digs; and they resonate powerfully with this setting, showing the human capacity to leave traces that serve as a bridge across time.

The same area also houses the *The Guardians* (2015). This video tells the story of the Catholic cemetery in Shkodër. Abandoned during the dictatorship, it became a site for encounters that would otherwise have been impossible; after the fall of the regime in 1991, it was refurbished, and has since spread out in an enthusiastic but chaotic way. It is now filled with a swarm of children who are paid to look after the tombs: a phenomenon that mirrors the country's contradictory but unstoppable rebirth.

The children's self-assurance also points to the many different possible facets of our relationship with life and death; their boundless energy hints at the urge for freedom that spurs human beings to break chains and overcome barriers; their efforts show them to be guardians of the future. The early Christian cemetery, where death dwells, is nevertheless a place full of life. And reflection on the hereafter may also offer a way to do better in the here-and-now. This work, humming with poetry and vitality, speaks delicately of the need to take care of the world around us, of new generations coming to the fore, of the dawning future, but also the possibility of forging a true, personal, concrete bond with the past; of establishing a means of transmission so that things of value can remain the shared heritage of those yet to come.

Paci's work grows out of a deep belief in art and its capacity to carve out spaces of reflection. The exactitude of his gaze, with its highly defined details and intense, recurring close ups, shows how contingency is not expunged from it, but rather filtered and boiled down to its essence. In this distillation, each work recreates the link between the deepest, most archaic dimension that lingers on in human behavior, sedimented in the images that art history has passed down to us; and the most immediate present, in which geopolitical dynamics have drastic repercussions on individual lives. The meaning of his work springs from this overlap between circumstance and universality, participation and distance, poetry and critique: a critique that becomes a constant assertion of the basic value of dignity, which can only be subjective and collective, moral and social at the same time. Paci's oeuvre thus fits seamlessly into the public discourse on the fundamental principles of respect, justice, and coexistence.

delinking and triangulating

by charles esche

While we can't guess what will become of the world, we can imagine what we would like it to become. The right to dream wasn't in the thirty rights of humans that the United Nations proclaimed at the end of 1948. But without it, without the right to dream and the waters that it gives to drink, the other rights would die of thirst.
Eduardo Galeano[1]

The Uruguayan writer and journalist Eduardo Galeano understood a lot about the power of suffering. He was a sometime exile who saw his brutalized continent languish under the boot of dictators for most of the twentieth century. Yet his writings always conjure up a potential for emancipation that lies beneath the pain. His resignation is always tainted with the possibility that things could be otherwise. Galeano seems an appropriate writer to cite in relation to the exhibition of Adrian Paci's work taking place in the Sant'Eustorgio Church in Milan. This exhibition likewise plays in a variety of ways with the balance between pain and liberation, reflecting the symbolic power of suffering and how it can be used to transform or transcend the immediate cause of the hurt.

The foundational work in the show, or at least for me the work from which the whole appears to depart, is *Rasha* (2017), a monumental screen image of a Syrian woman set to an Arabic-language audio track. The woman, Rasha, is not the one speaking, but rather she is listening, together with us, to her own disembodied voice talking back to her. She nods tensely, smiles, or looks puzzled as she recognizes the story being told. Unable to understand Arabic, I am compelled to look at her face closely. One of her eyes is clouded, possibly the result of some previous violence. The other eye peers out nervously. Her neck is taut, and she often looks down and away, hiding herself in her own thoughts. The effect is all the stronger in the Dominican refectory of the basilica, surrounded by Roman Catholic oil paintings—slightly generic renderings of the Christian myth that include a number of full-face images of Mary, mother of Jesus. Looking across from painting to screen, it is hard not to recognize that the Christian Mary could also easily be described as a suffering woman from exactly the same geography.

This coincidence of silent, pained faces separated in time by two thousand years sets up the expectations and the potentiality of the exhibition as a whole. It is made in and for a site that is both a museum and

1 Eduardo Galeano from a lecture on the right to dream, https://www.youtube.com/watch?v=T1XqTBNxLys.

a working Christian temple. The Basilica di Sant'Eustorgio is the oldest Christian site in Milan. For a time, it held the relics of the Three Magi, and it is still an important pilgrimage stop on the route to Rome. It is a significant site for artworks by an Albanian-born artist who was educated in art within an official atheist society that rejected Christianity, Islam, and modernity but later collapsed through its own contradictions, and therefore no longer represents a position that the artist has to defend or oppose as an a priori condition of making work.

The independence from both religion and ideology that this unusual background represents for Paci is what creates a different possibility in this unequivocally Christian situation. Above all, it permits the intention of the works to step outside the known parameters of how art and religion engage with each other. The artistic images, based on the biography of their author, do not have to carry the burden of illustrating a canonical story or affirming the doctrines of faith; but nor are they forced to reject the tenets of that faith in order to shape their own discourse. Paci's distance from religion, combined with the failure of his original dogmatic atheism, gives him the possibility to exhibit in this church without the burden of competing with it, staying true to being ambivalent about faith—religious or modernist. If we place the exhibition in the context of the decolonial thought that is, I believe, crucial to understanding where the world is today, we could say that this exhibition is an exemplary moment of delinking in which the predetermined lines of connection between material and immaterial phenomena are broken—or at least sufficiently loosened—to allow new connections to be forged (or relinked, as decolonial theory would describe it).

To make this clear, here is Walter Mignolo, one of the leading decolonial thinkers:

> *The global political society has organized itself in myriad ways because neither the State nor the Market has taken care of them. The recasting of spirituality plays an important role here. We know that religion has many faces, and I will not go into this now, but simply mention that significant sectors of religions, different religions in different parts of the world, are joining the political society without abandoning their religious foundations. One of the tasks is to decolonize religion so as to liberate spirituality.*[2]

2 Walter Mignolo in an interview with Christopher Mattison, *Critical Legal Thinking*, May 2, 2012, http://criticallegalthinking.com/2012/05/02/delinking-decoloniality-dewesternization-interview-with-walter-mignolo-part-ii/.

In these terms, placing Rasha next to Mary is just such an act of decolonizing religion. Both women, strong, graceful, vulnerable, and mysterious, are thus potentially freed from the prejudices that entrap them—the "Mother of God" just as much as the "Syrian refugee"—to once again become political and spiritual beings.

This method of incorporating the environment of the church in order to delink both the work and the surrounding ecclesiastical architecture from its familiar context is revisited frequently in the exhibition. The repetitive structure of delinking and relinking not only confirms its own effectiveness but also allows a third, more materialist element to enter into the equation. The sculpture *Home to Go* (2001) is placed directly on the floor in front of a crucifix, underneath which are two statues of donors to the church, one holding a small model of a church in his left hand. In Paci's sculpture, the life-size figure resembling the artist carries what looks like the heavy burden of an upturned tiled roof on his back. Hard work, effort, and sacrifice are depicted here, both in the Christ figure on the cross and in the artist carrying his roof. The reference to the Christian story of Jesus carrying his cross through the streets of Jerusalem is obvious, but the donor figure in the background also suggests that maybe the roof could offer collective protection from the elements. This conversation between the existing elements of the church and the new work is rich in itself, creating a new visibility for the decorations of the basilica and drawing attention to what might otherwise appear unremarkable or predictably affirmative of the main Christian narrative given its site in a Catholic temple.

Other elements construct an equally complicated process of delinking and relinking in the way that Rasha and Mary did. Surrounding the crucifix already mentioned are a series of beautifully installed display cases showing the silvered treasures of the church with their individual dedications to God and His servants. As a background to the depiction of redemptive poverty in both the Christ figure and Paci's sculpture, they set off a train of connections in which the attractions of and contradictions between material wealth and spiritual purity are the only possible subject. Both the body on the crucifix and the figure carrying the roof are dressed in loincloths. The richness of the environment jars all the more with these suffering bodies in a way that speaks of unrewarded labor as a direct contrast to the luxury of the Roman Catholic appurtenances.[3] If we again remember Paci's socialist education in Albania, we might see

3 As an aside, it is tempting to see in this Dominican monastery a very Catholic dispute played out between the mendicant order and their opposite number in the Franciscans, with the latter's insistence on communal property and private deprivation.

not only the gap between the spiritual and the religious as spelled out by Mignolo, but also a third materialist understanding of the world in which social or cultural actions are determined by actual material conditions, or, as Karl Marx wrote in *The German Ideology*, "The nature of individuals thus depends on the material conditions determining their production."[4] Here, three competing ideologies are laid out before us in a triangulated spatial configuration that is remarkable for not obviously choosing any side, or at least for understanding that nothing would be less persuasive here than another didactic exegesis of good and bad ethics.

Elsewhere, the moves of delinking play out in increasingly complex ways. Excavations below the undercroft of the basilica in the nineteenth century revealed a third- or fourth-century Christian burial ground that is now open to the public. The inscriptions on the graves reveal in part a clandestine, persecuted faith, for which its followers sacrificed themselves. In the midst of this artificially maintained cemetery, Paci has placed a short film of children in his hometown of Shkoder, who are shown hanging around in an abandoned Christian cemetery. The literal parallels are of course obvious, but this goes further than speaking of Christian persecution and the fictions of archaeology, and touches on the worship of death that is an essential part of Christianity. As the film unfolds, we see more and more children washing the graves in something that suggests a collective cleansing ritual, and in this context it is hard not to read it as an atoning for sins. Perhaps we are witnessing a spontaneous reburial in the light of contemporary Albanians being again permitted to worship their gods publicly. The background information that this cemetery was abandoned for a long time during the Communist regime and has only recently been given some official status again adds to the sense of making something right or relinking past and present.

Two other non-video works in the exhibition add an extra element into the triangulated delinking in which religion, spirituality, and materialism configure themselves around one another and add time and history even more clearly to the mix. The first is a series of photographs called *The Encounter* (2011), shot in an ill-defined space in front of a Baroque church in the Sicilian town of Scicli. In it the artist stands by a chair and individually greets every resident of the town as they form a huge queue around the church square. This gesture of the stranger-artist doing the greeting is already intriguing. When it is combined, as here, with a specific location and the prejudices about Sicilians as closed and

4 Karl Marx, *The German Ideology*, chapter 1A, originally published 1845, https://www.marxists.org/archive/marx/works/1845/german-ideology/ch01a.htm.

secretive, as well as within the beautifully decadent scenography of the urban Mediterranean environment, the sequence of photographs becomes a triangular play with place, history, and contemporaneity within a context that initially appears unchanged and unchanging for centuries. One suspects a summoning of historical ghosts here, in the sense of how Sicily is often portrayed as subject to powerful external forces against which the Mafia and the Catholic Church serve as convenient shields. In this light, we might be a little suspicious of the genuineness of the exchange, or at least of aspects of public ritual and the importance of being seen to have done something as opposed to only doing it. At the same time, this ritual of welcome might be a way of opening up to new arrivals and introducing a new form of liturgy to the very topical process of displacement and migration. There, in Milan's Sant'Eustorgio, of course there are other internal Italian resonances of northern occupation and southern resistance that spill out from this work into the surrounding space.

The final piece I would like to discuss is called *Brothers* (2010) and is perhaps the most quotidian in the exhibition. A framed grayscale mosaic standing on the floor, rather like a projection screen, it resolves at a distance into an image of two boys sitting alone and very closely together in a mundane rural landscape. The boys stare intensely out of the image—their eyes are some of the darkest stones. Placed against an ornate metal screen, the mosaic recalls Byzantine forms of ecclesiastical image making that predate the surrounding paintings and sculptures. It translates the image into a monumental one using a medium that can hardly not be read in symbolic or metaphorical terms. We are then faced with a puzzle. The use of grayscale most obviously recalls black-and-white photography and therefore suggests a time in the late nineteenth or early twentieth century, while the technique could make it much earlier or much later. In the fragmented faces of the two children, it is quite hard not to see a reflection of the crimes against humanity that run through the last hundred years. Knowing that the image might have a much more innocent source in a country wedding challenges the sense of foreboding but doesn't remove it. Like the spirituality and material of earlier works, *Brothers* carries all of this and more within the image. Galeano's right to dream does not solve any of these existential puzzles, but, like water, without it (without this art) humans would not have a life worth the name.

adrian paci, the guardians

chiostri di sant'eustorgio
28.03–01.10.2017

all images / tutte le immagini:
photo credit / credito
fotografico: andrea rossetti

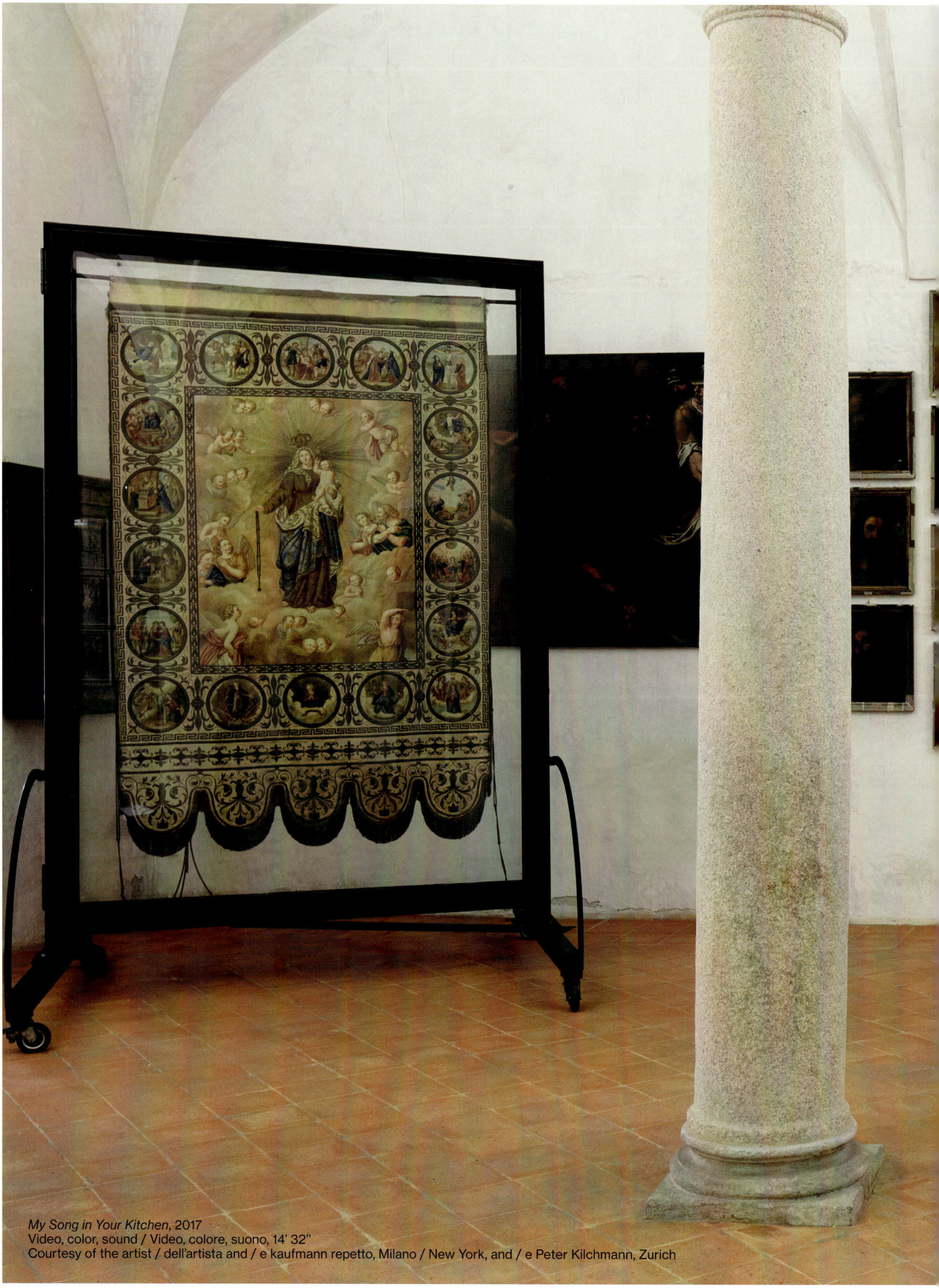

My Song in Your Kitchen, 2017
Video, color, sound / Video, colore, suono, 14' 32"
Courtesy of the artist / dell'artista and / e kaufmann repetto, Milano / New York, and / e Peter Kilchmann, Zurich

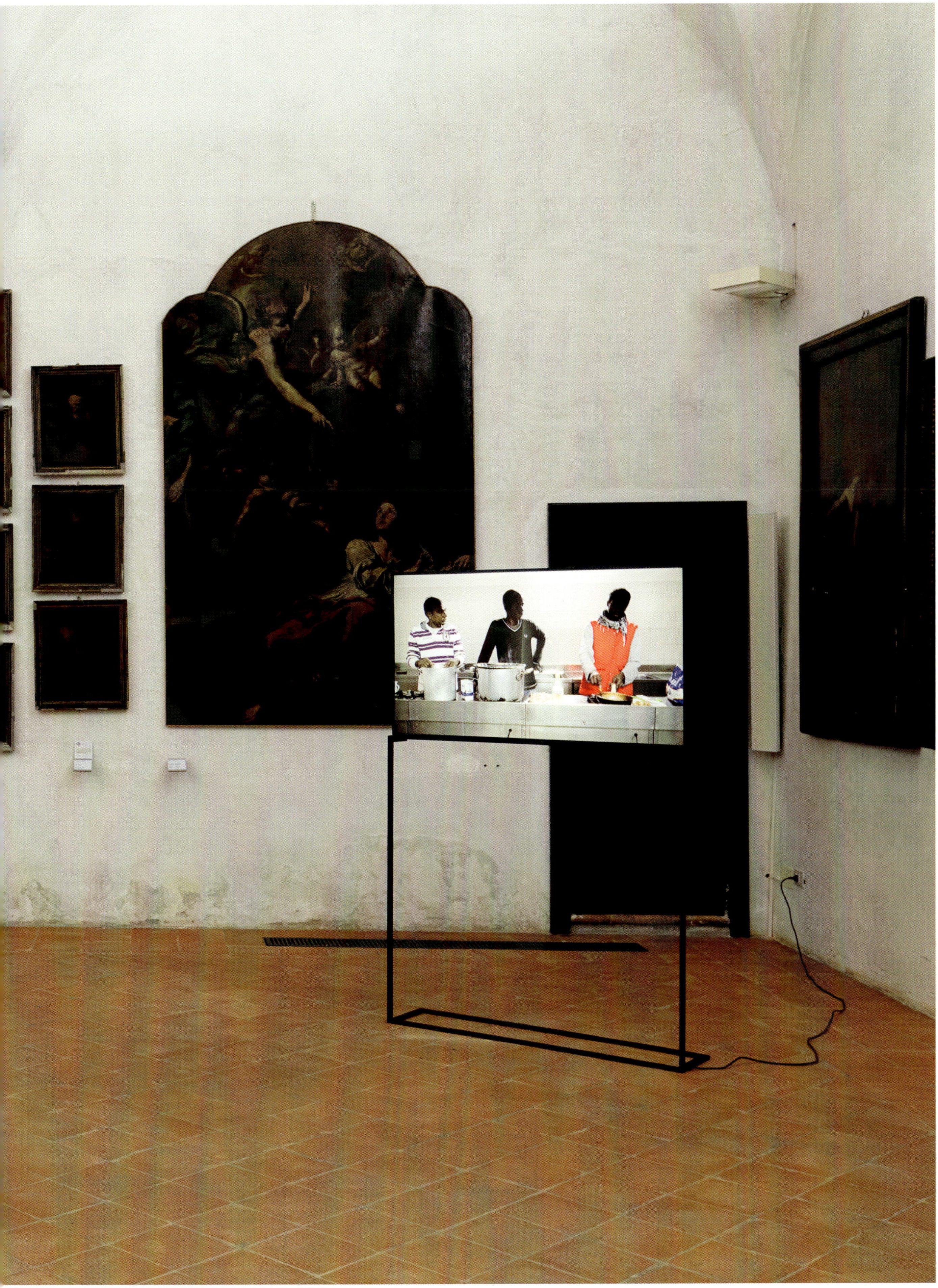

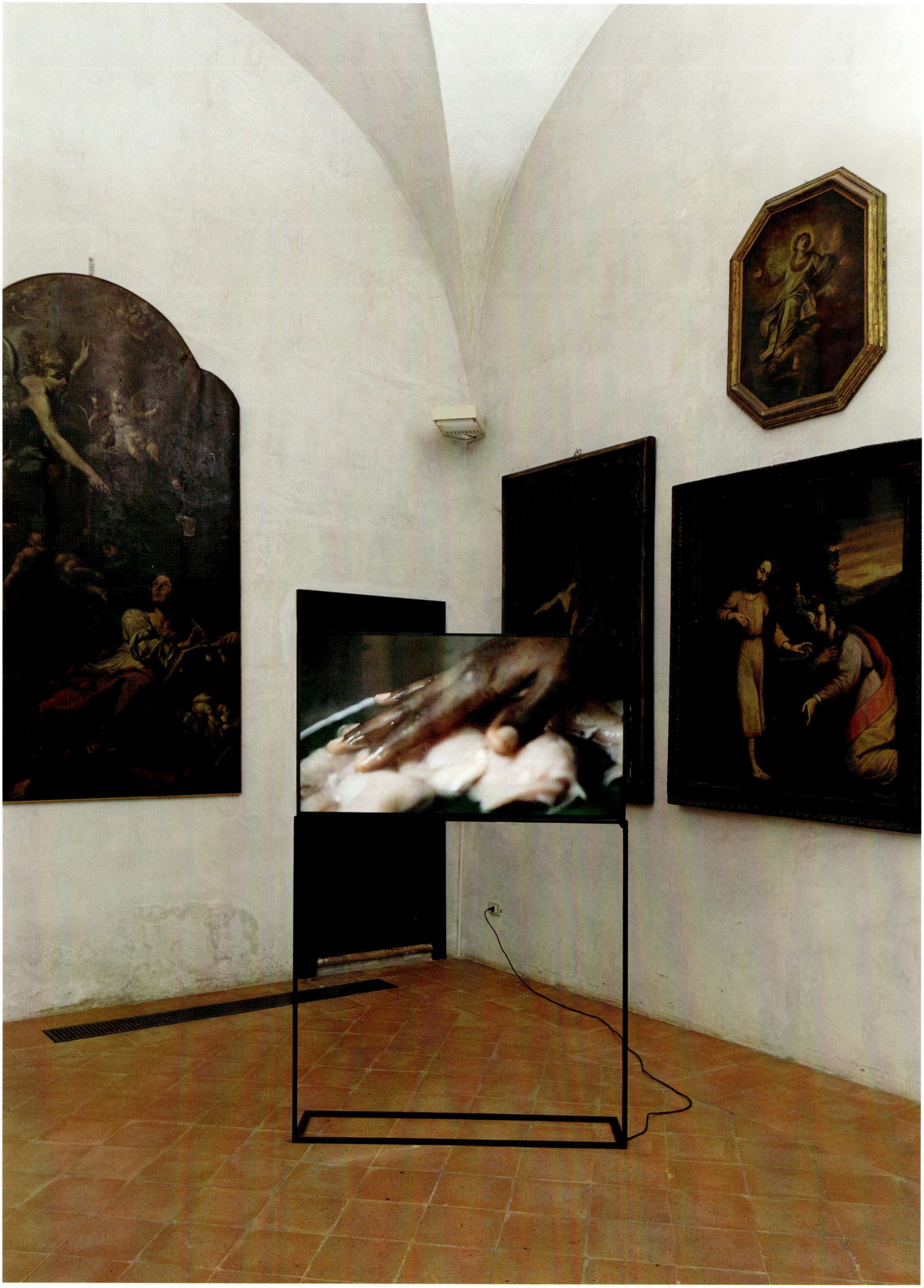

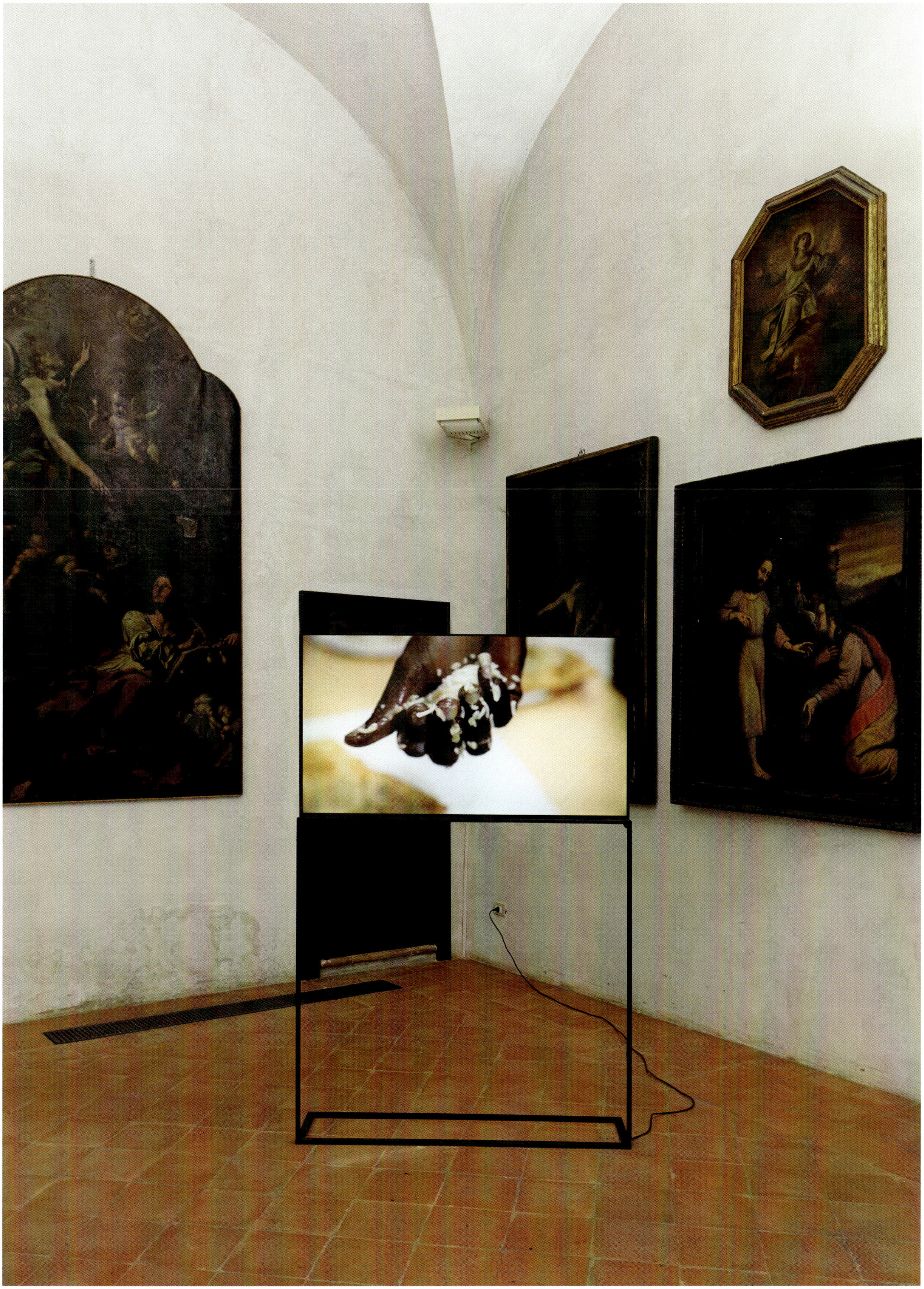

The Line, 2007
Framed photograph / Fotografia incorniciata, 60 × 74,5 cm
Courtesy of the artist / dell'artista and / e kaufmann repetto, Milano / New York, and / e Peter Kilchmann, Zurich

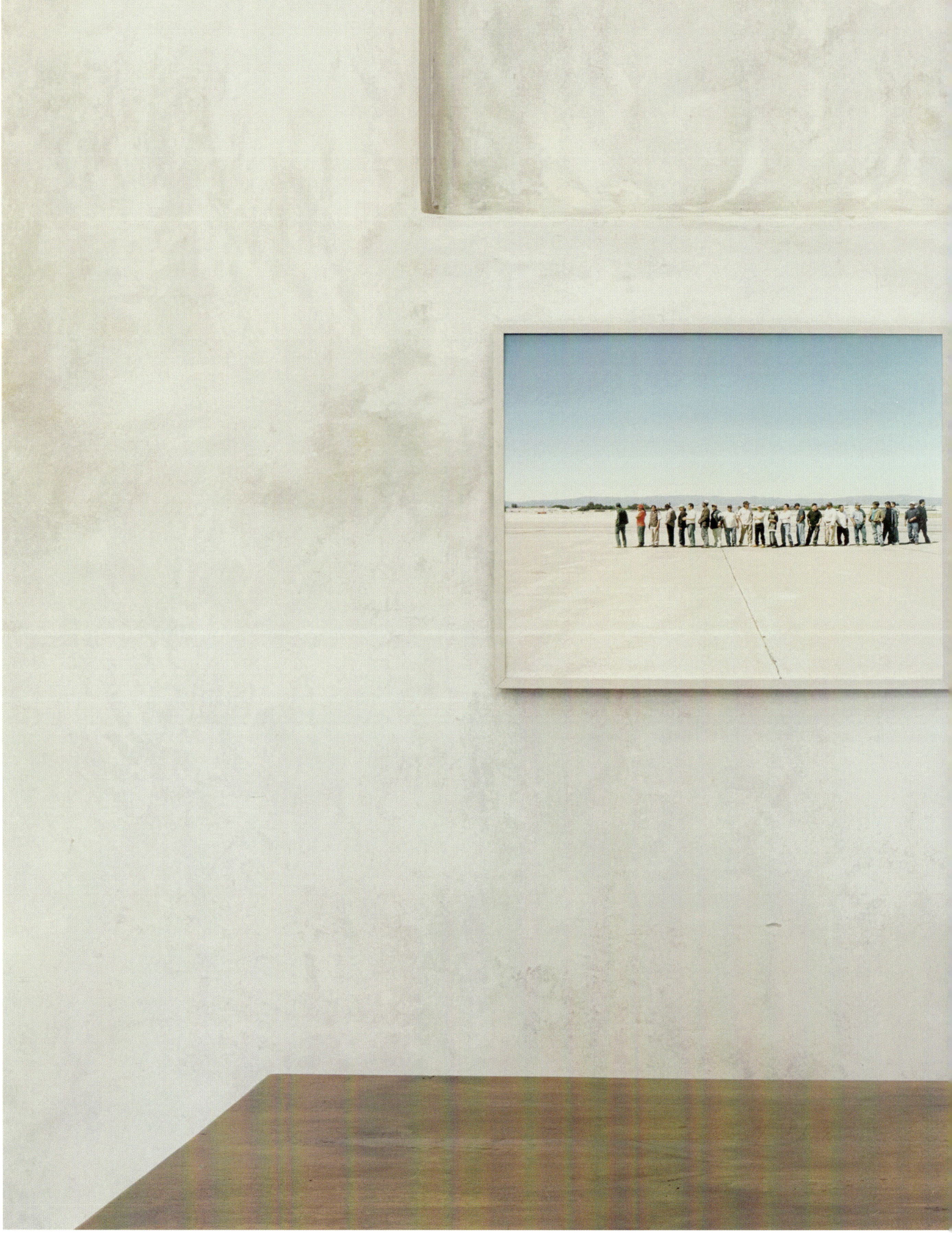

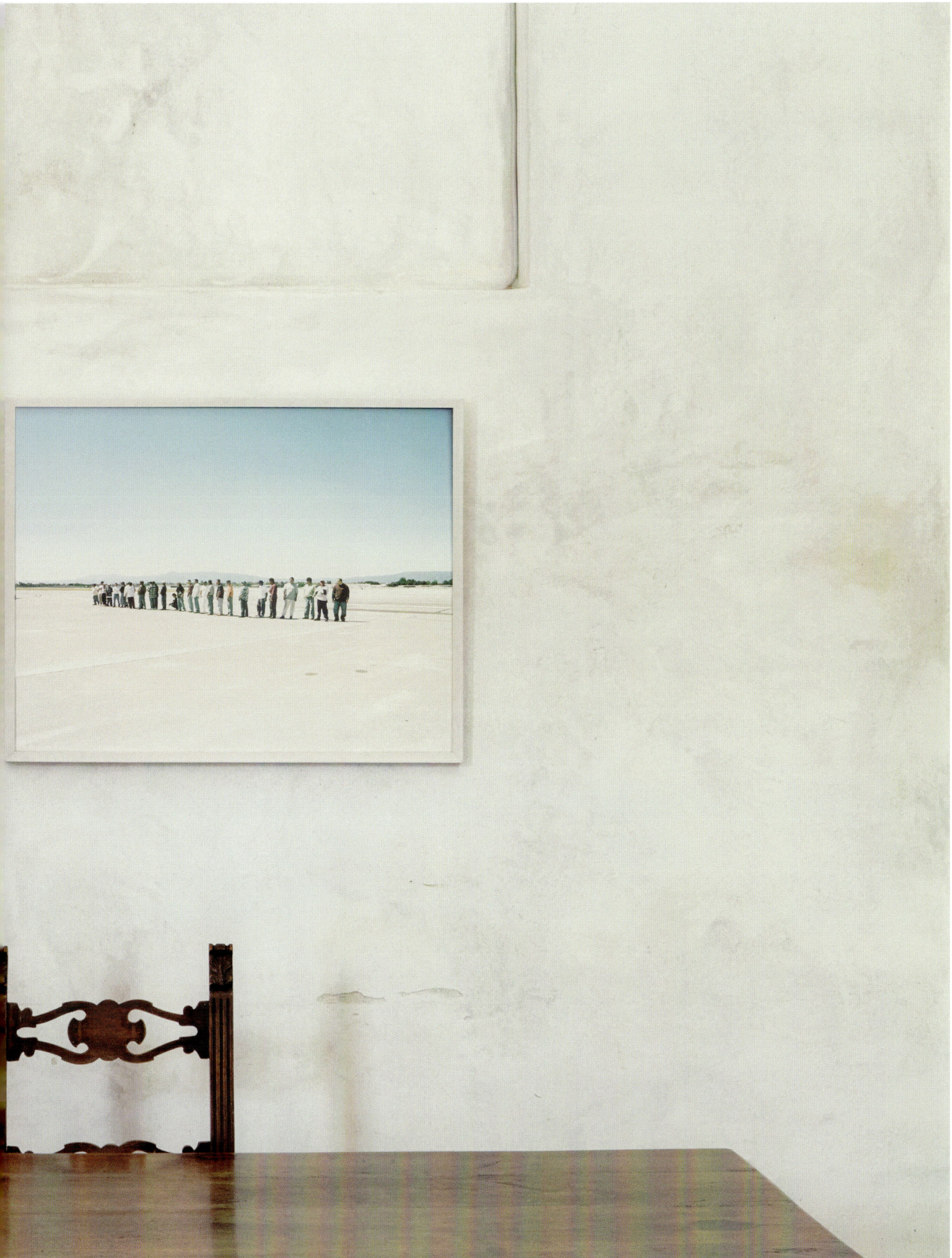

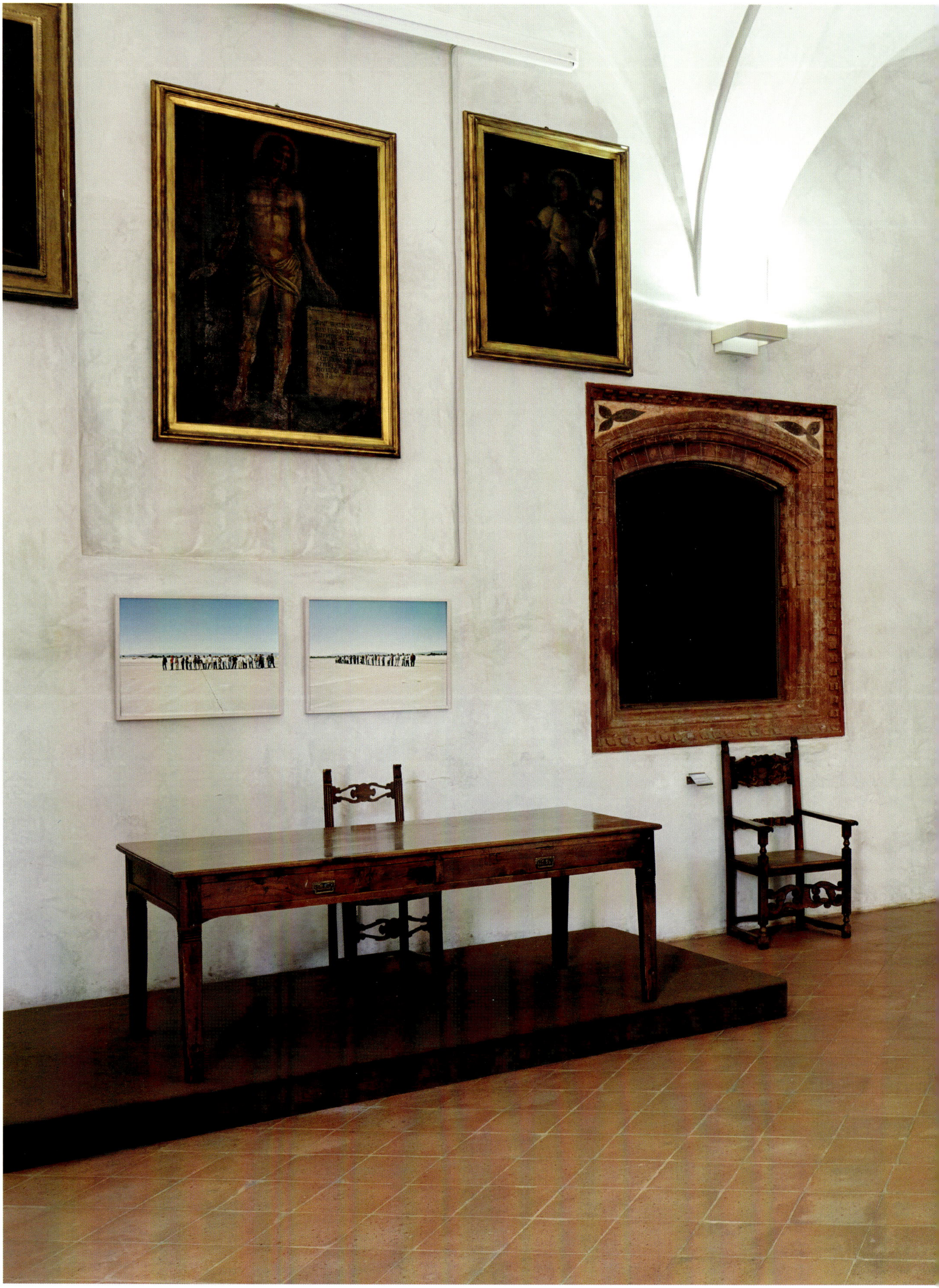

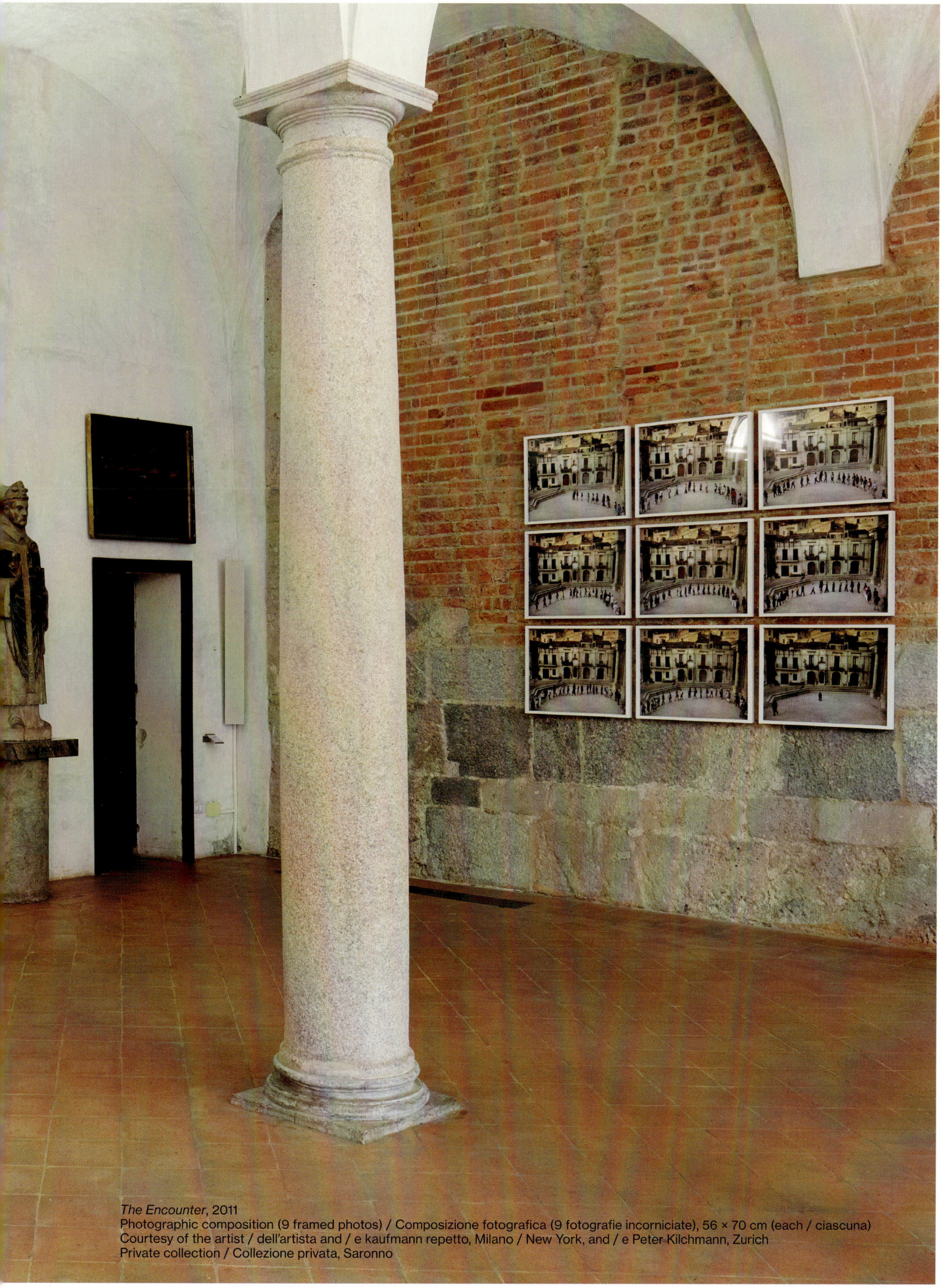

The Encounter, 2011
Photographic composition (9 framed photos) / Composizione fotografica (9 fotografie incorniciate), 56 × 70 cm (each / ciascuna)
Courtesy of the artist / dell'artista and / e kaufmann repetto, Milano / New York, and / e Peter Kilchmann, Zurich
Private collection / Collezione privata, Saronno

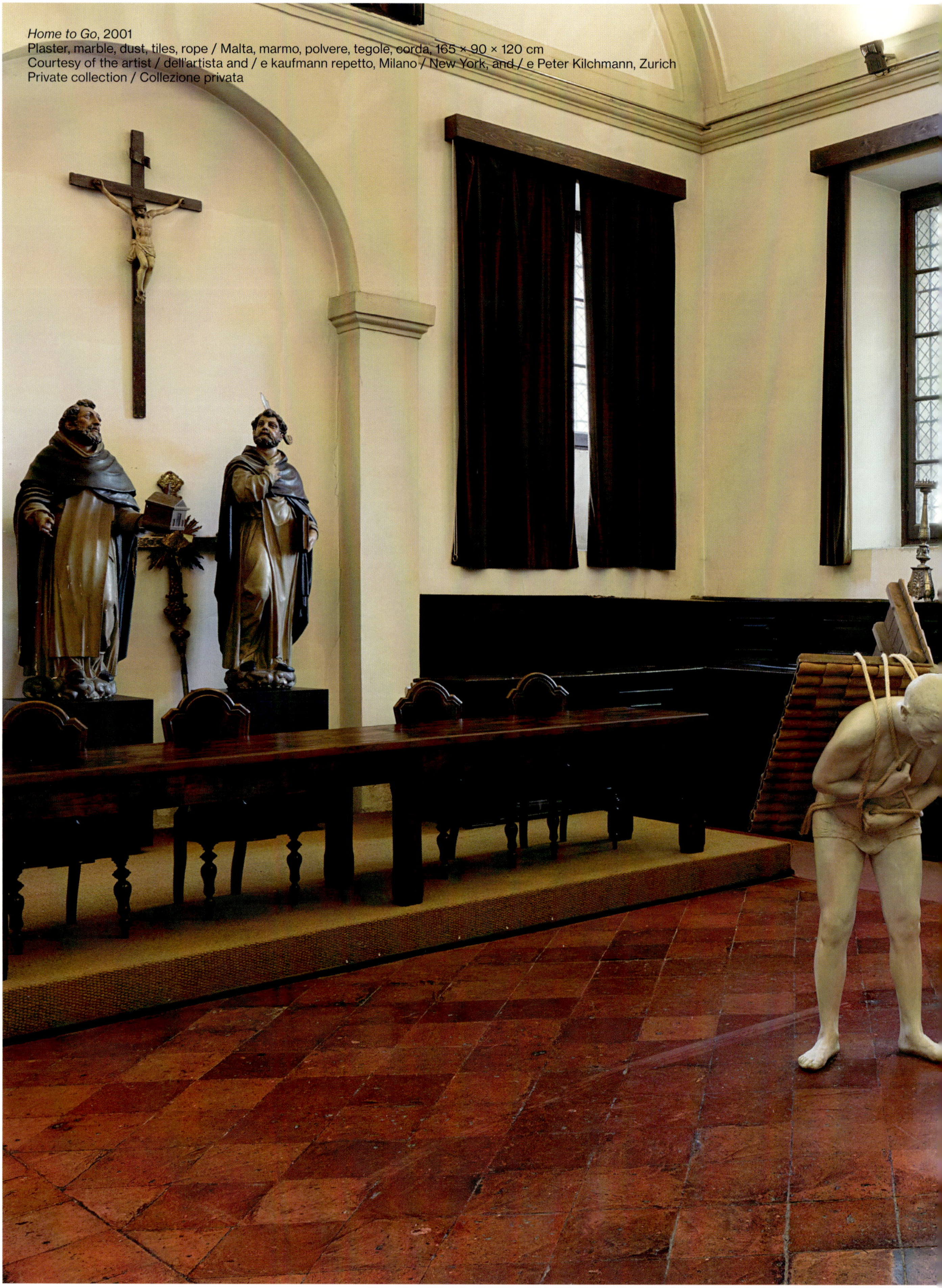

Home to Go, 2001
Plaster, marble, dust, tiles, rope / Malta, marmo, polvere, tegole, corda, 165 × 90 × 120 cm
Courtesy of the artist / dell'artista and / e kaufmann repetto, Milano / New York, and / e Peter Kilchmann, Zurich
Private collection / Collezione privata

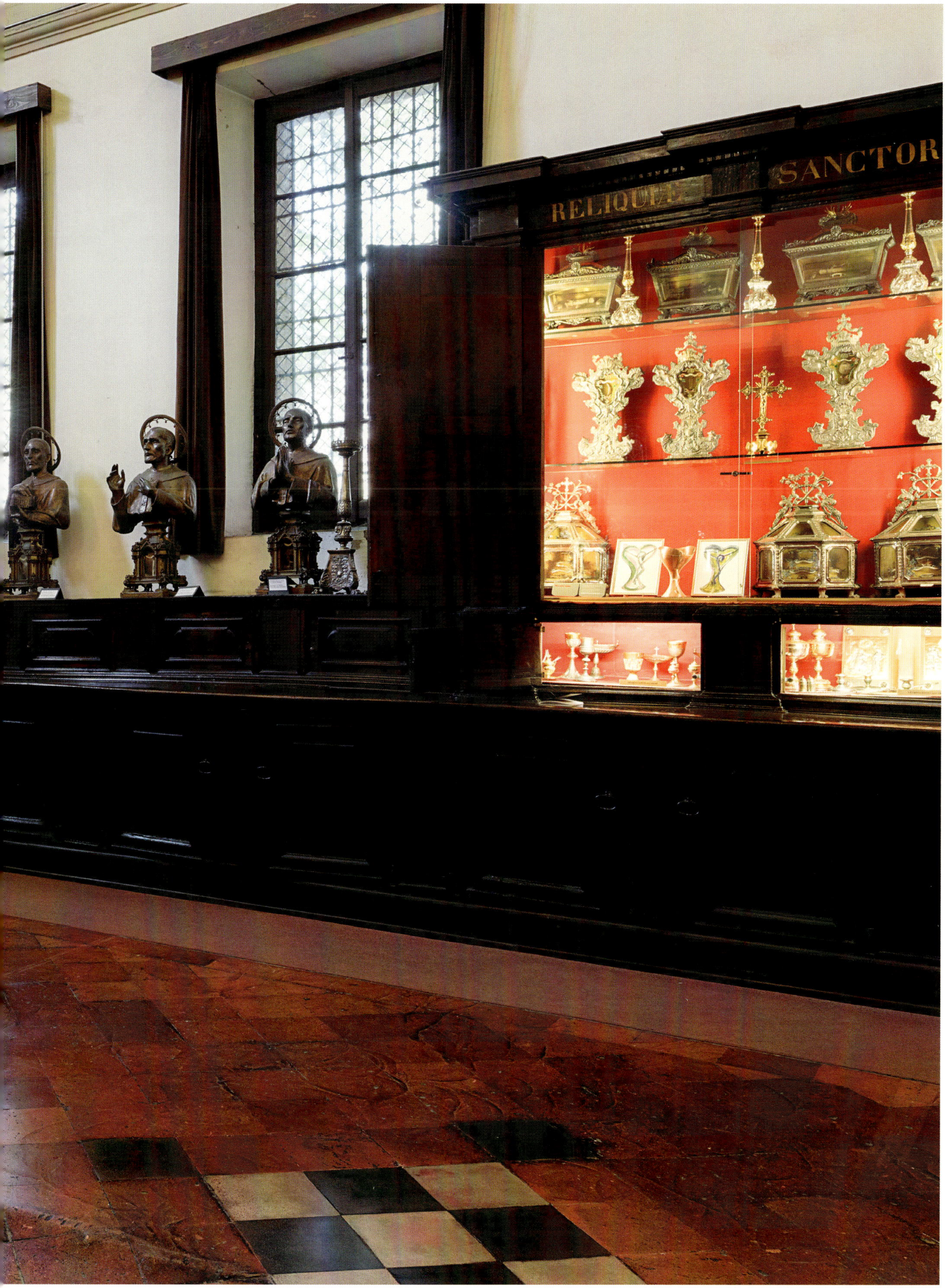
RELIQUI
SANCTOR

Klodi, 2005
Film on / su DVD, 40'
Courtesy of the artist / dell'artista
and / e kaufmann repetto, Milano / New York,
and / e Peter Kilchmann, Zurich

Brothers, 2010
Marble mosaic on wood / Mosaico di marmo su legno,
150 × 183 cm
Courtesy of the artist / dell'artista
and / e kaufmann repetto, Milano / New York,
and / e Peter Kilchmann, Zurich

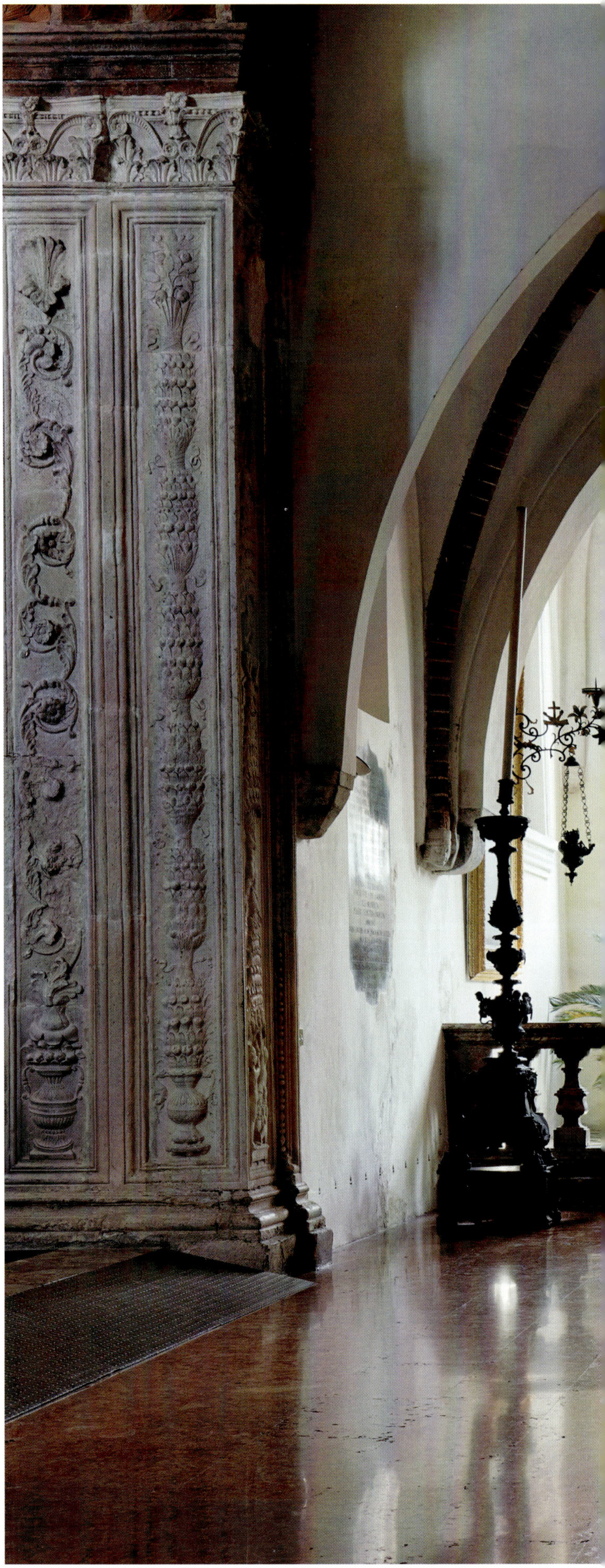

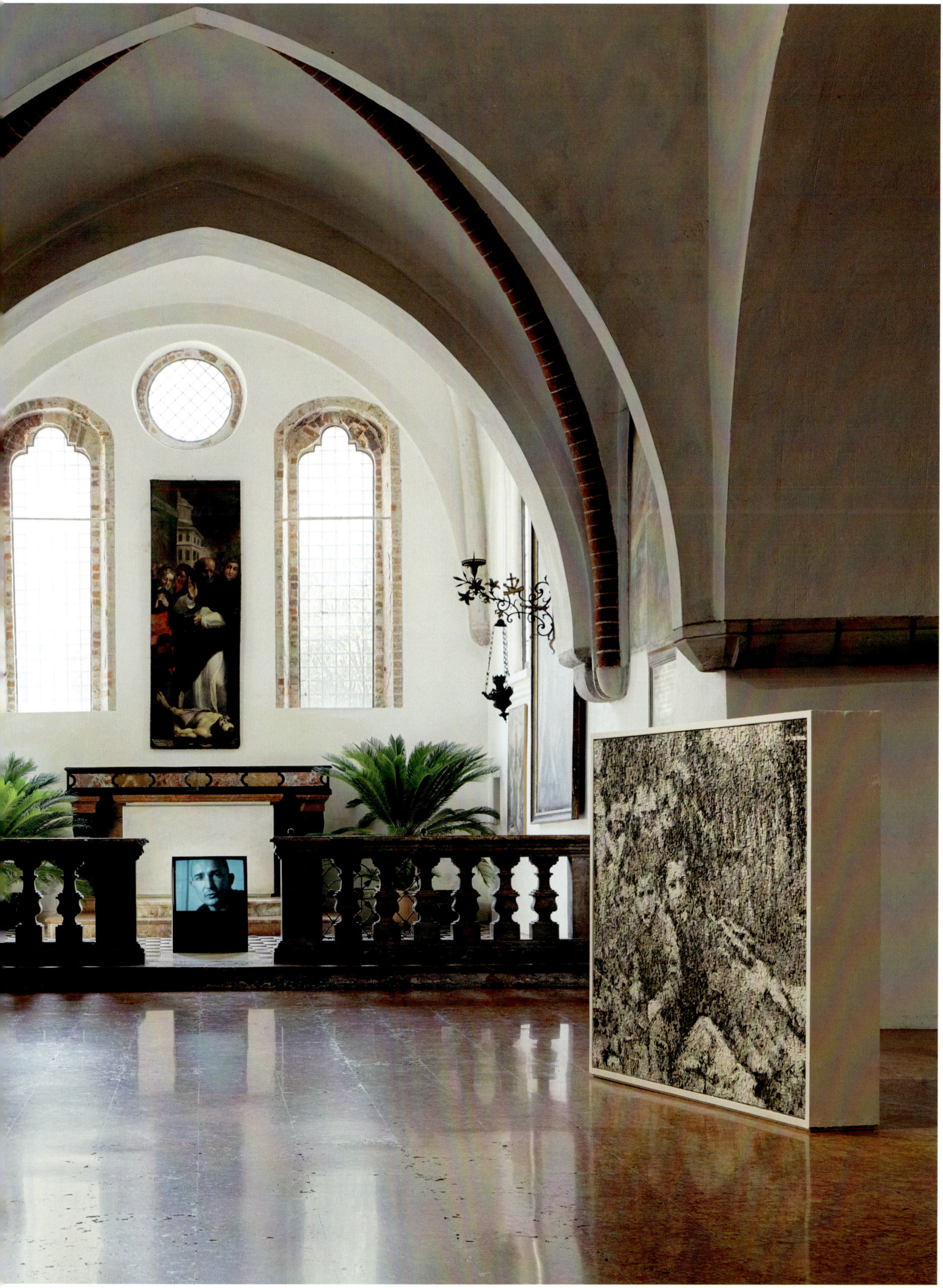

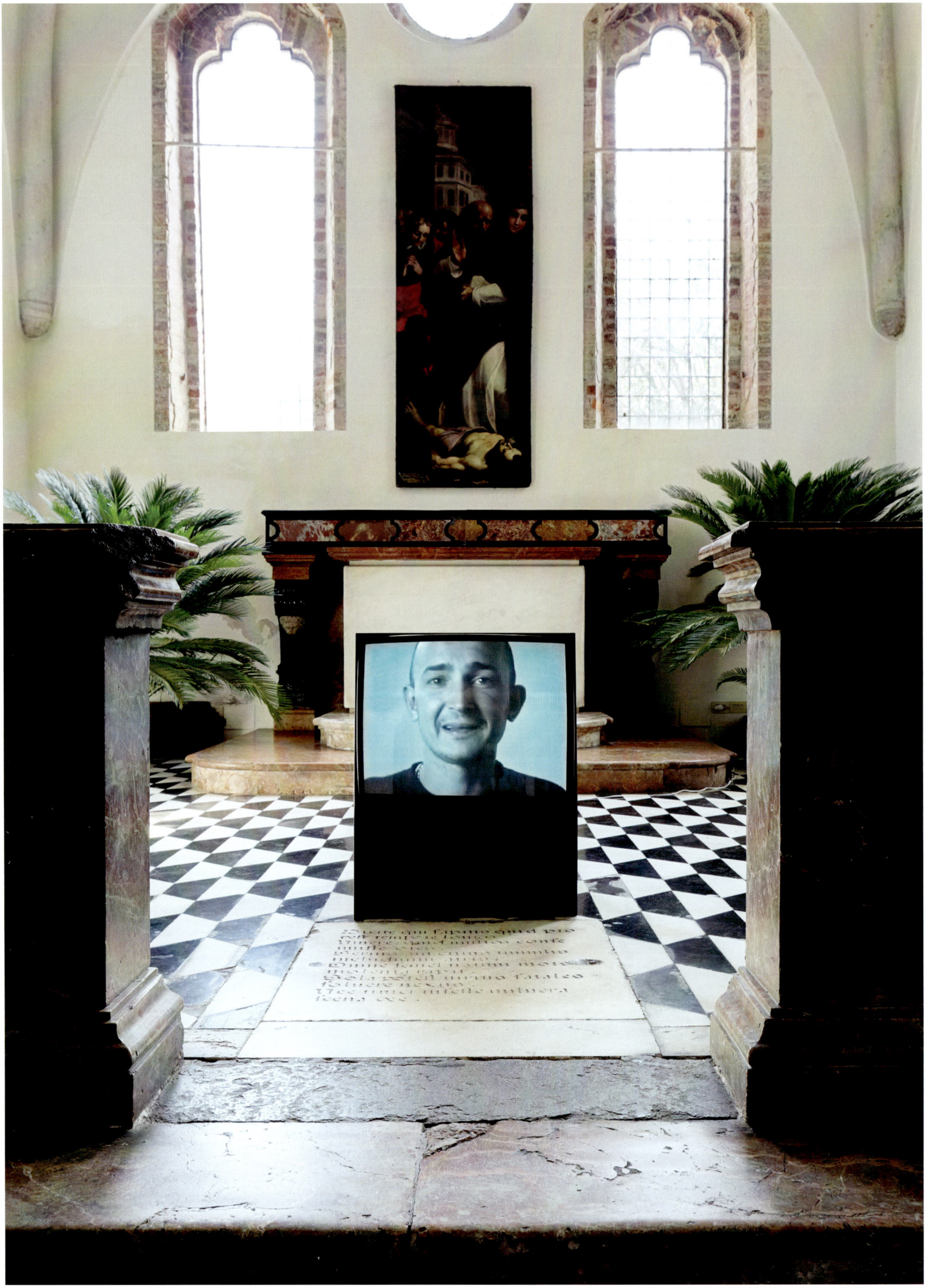

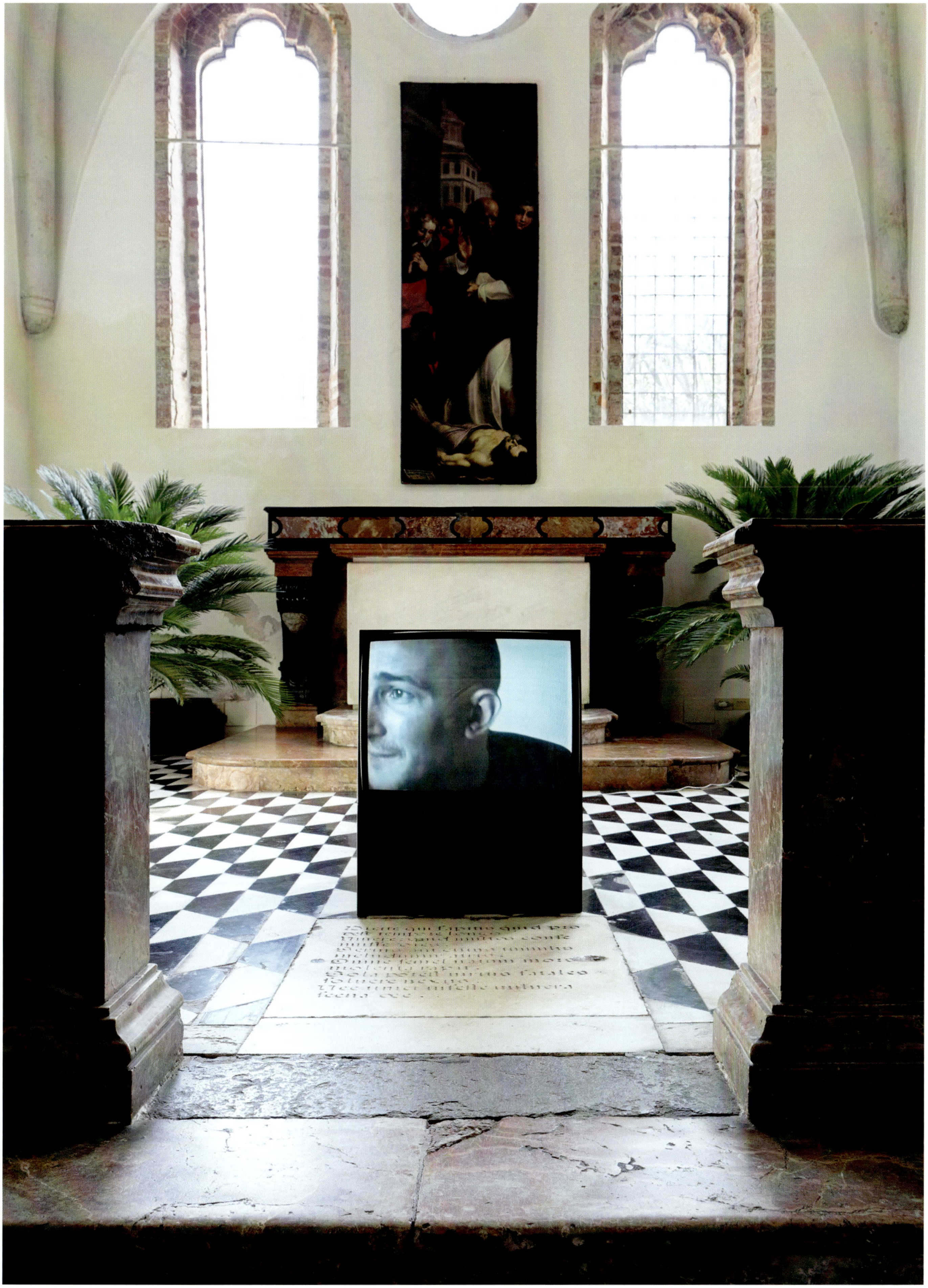

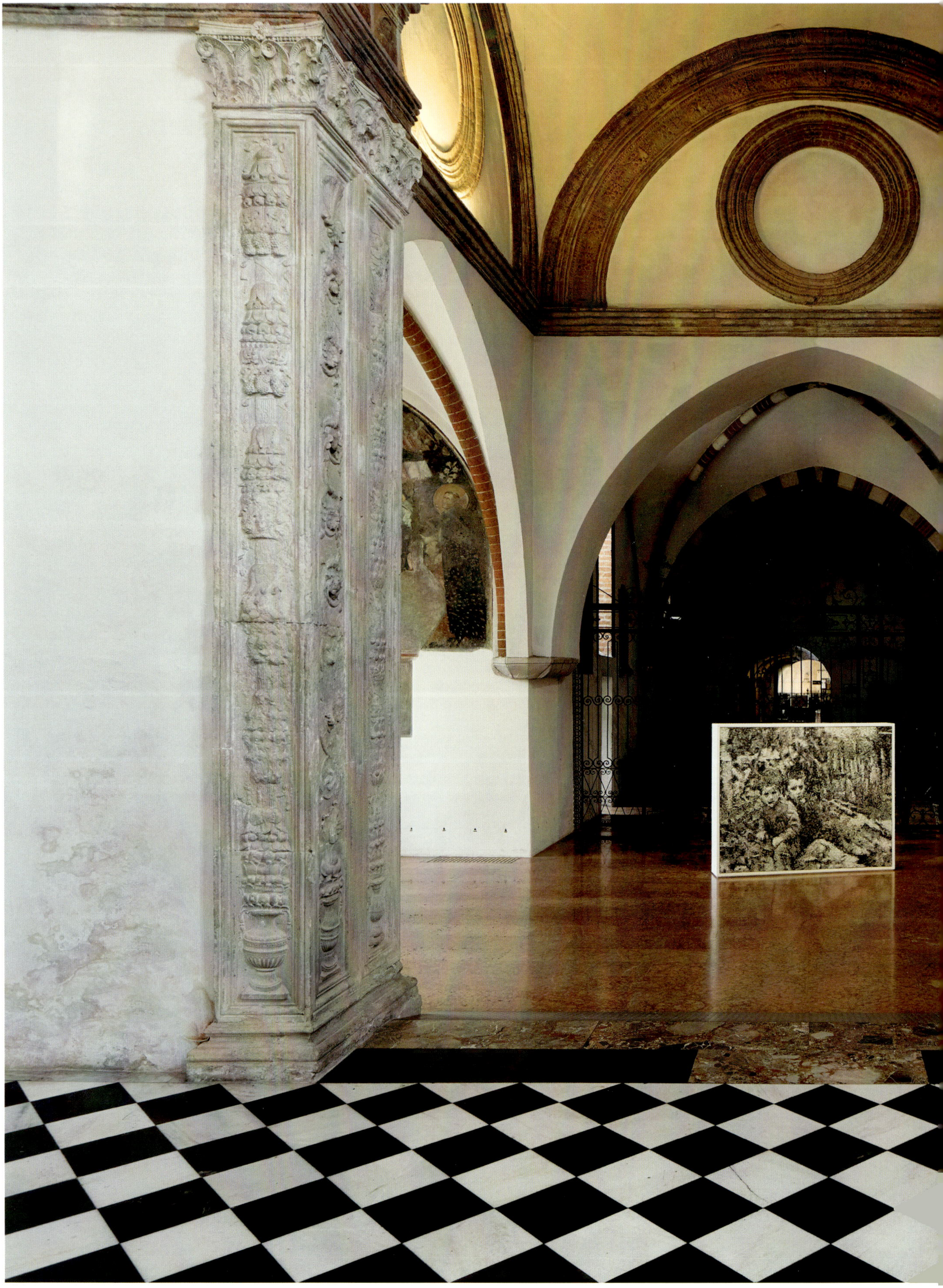

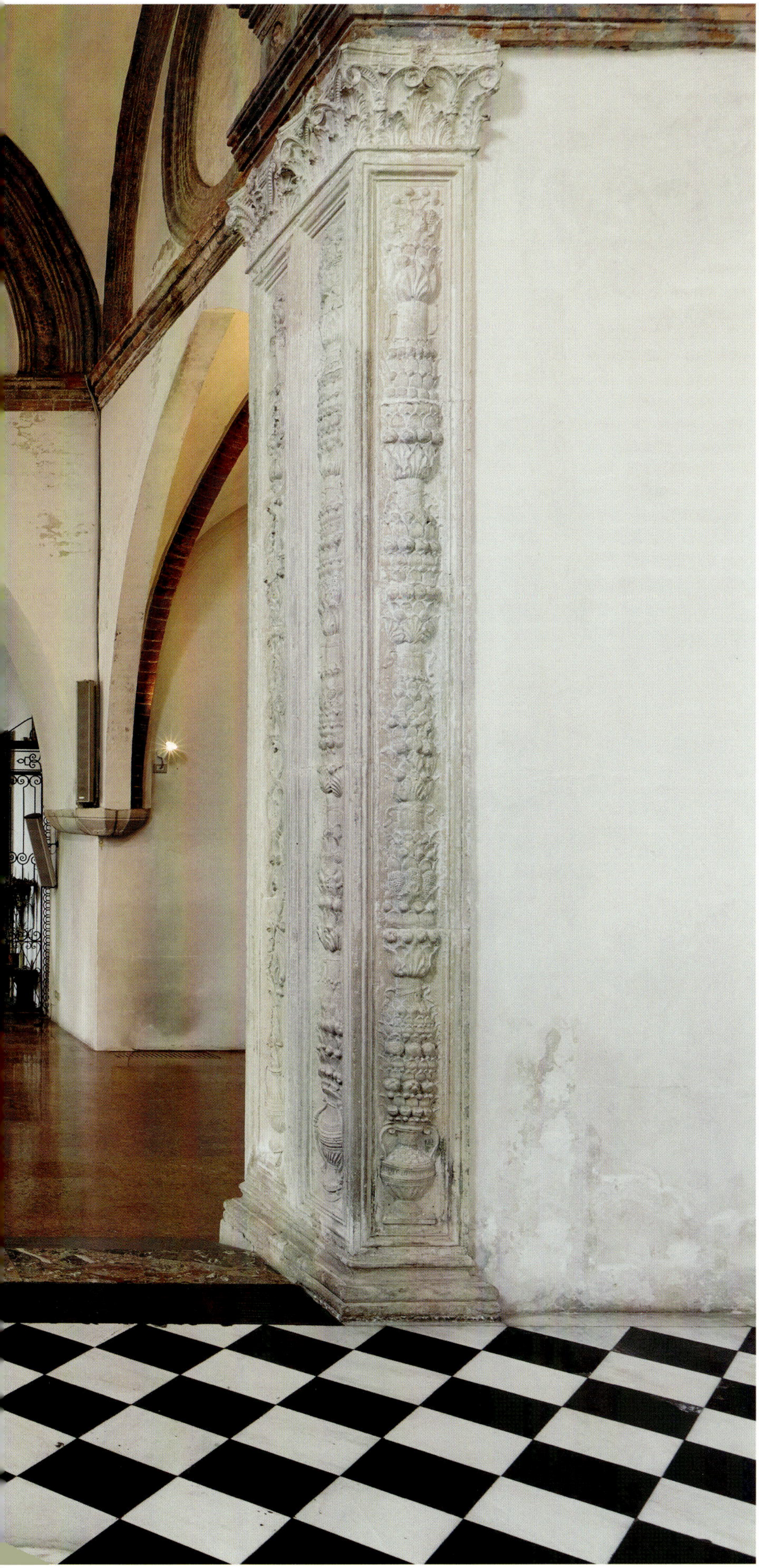

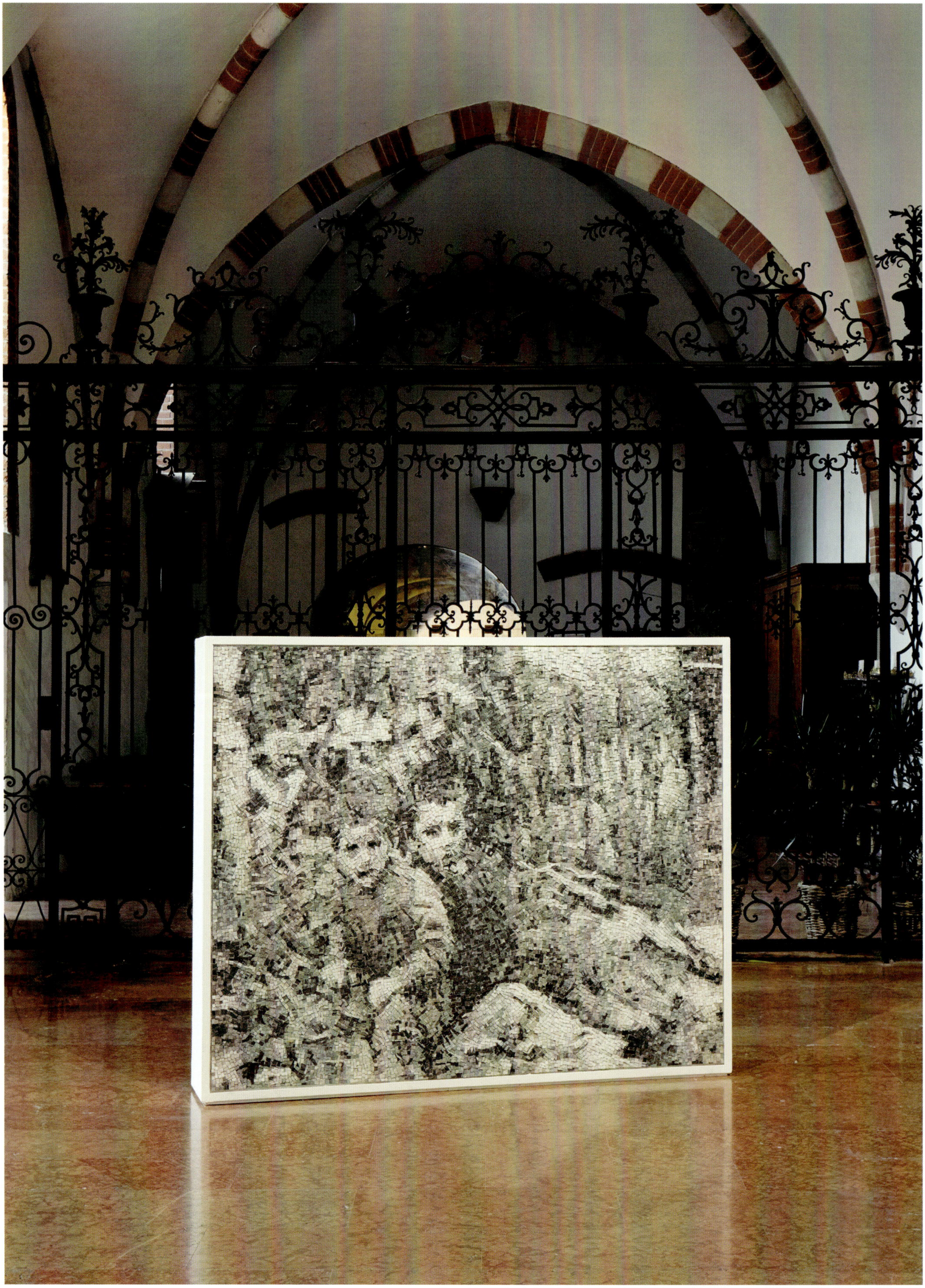

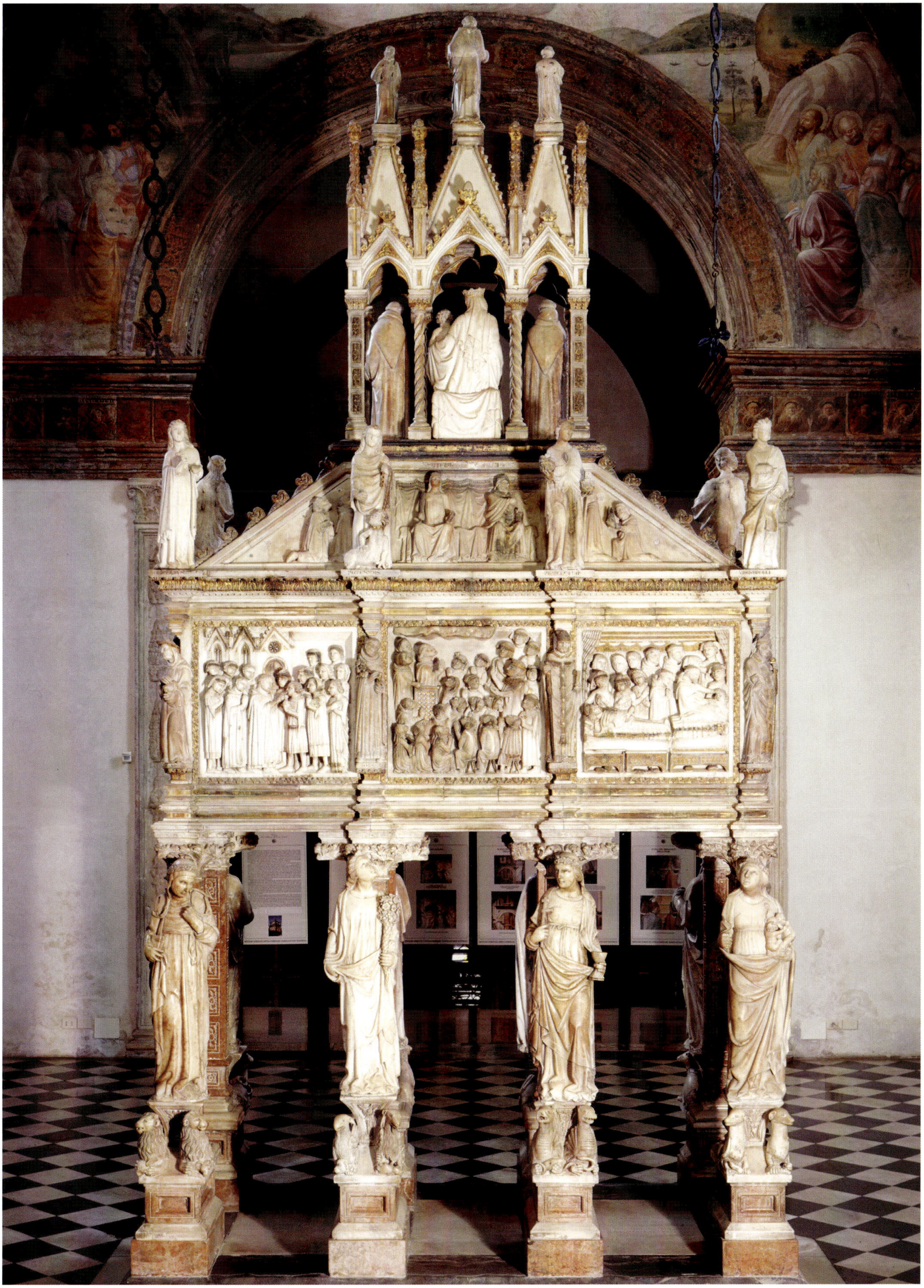

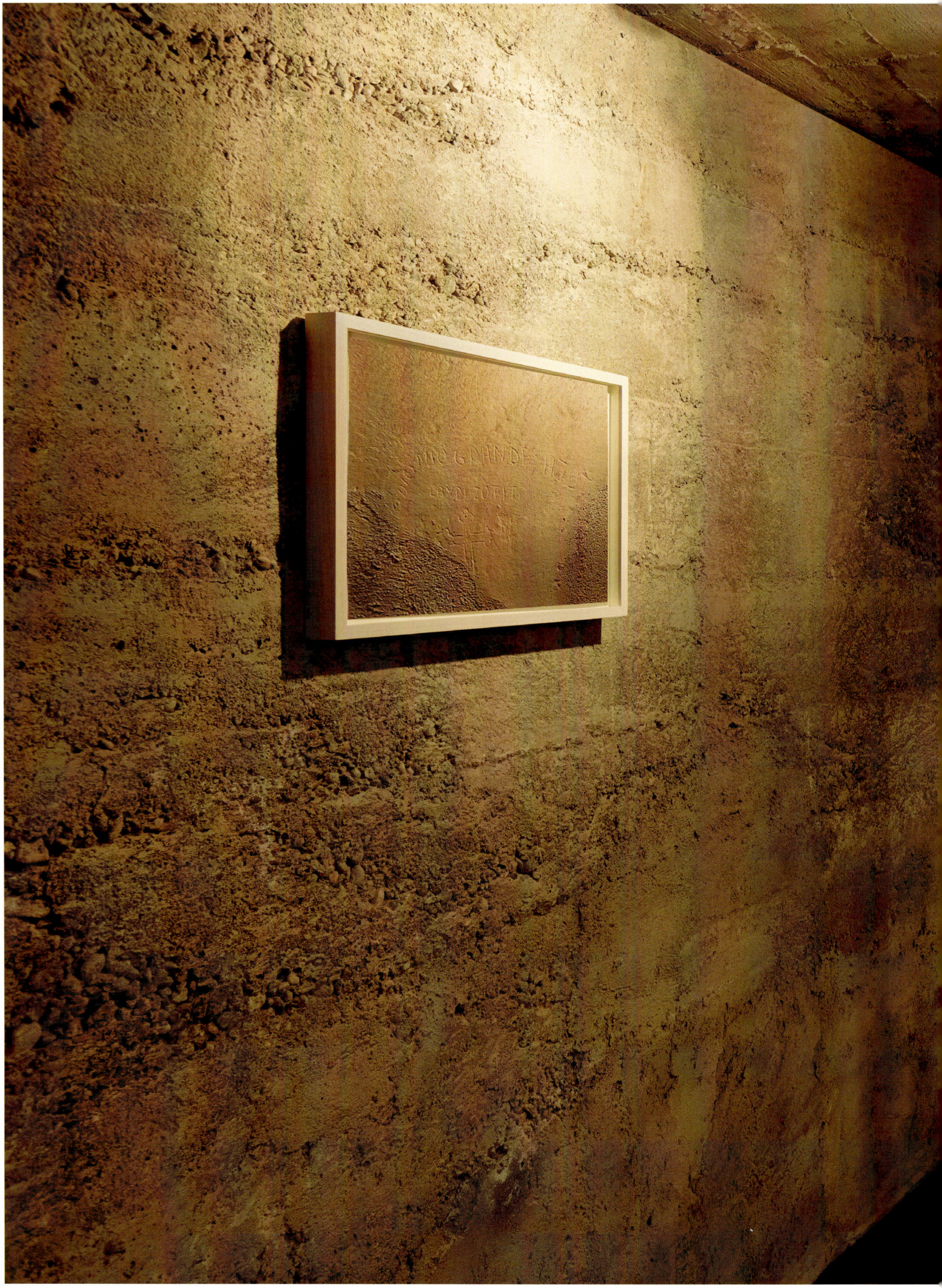

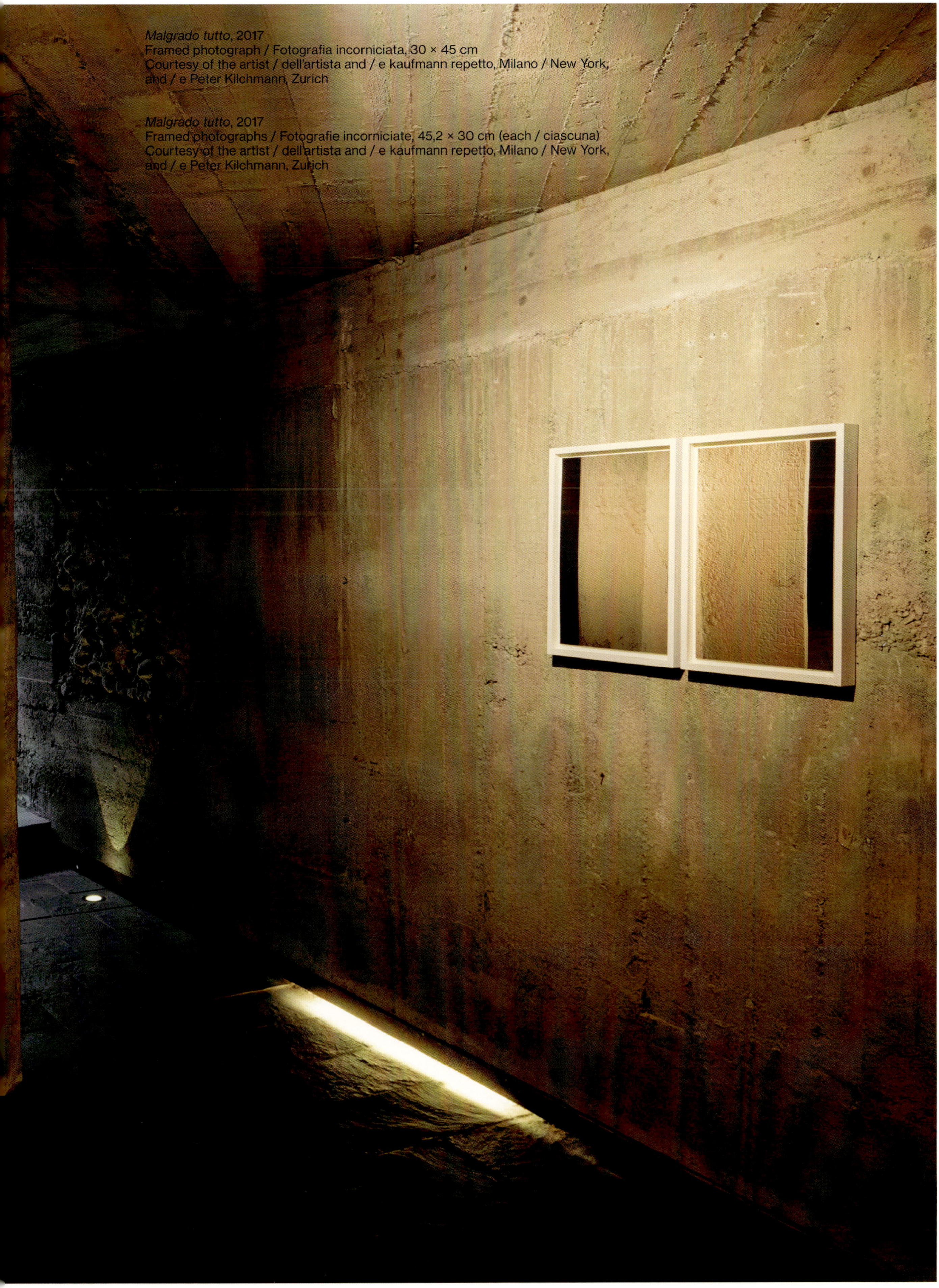

Malgrado tutto, 2017
Framed photograph / Fotografia incorniciata, 30 × 45 cm
Courtesy of the artist / dell'artista and / e kaufmann repetto, Milano / New York, and / e Peter Kilchmann, Zurich

Malgrado tutto, 2017
Framed photographs / Fotografie incorniciate, 45,2 × 30 cm (each / ciascuna)
Courtesy of the artist / dell'artista and / e kaufmann repetto, Milano / New York, and / e Peter Kilchmann, Zurich

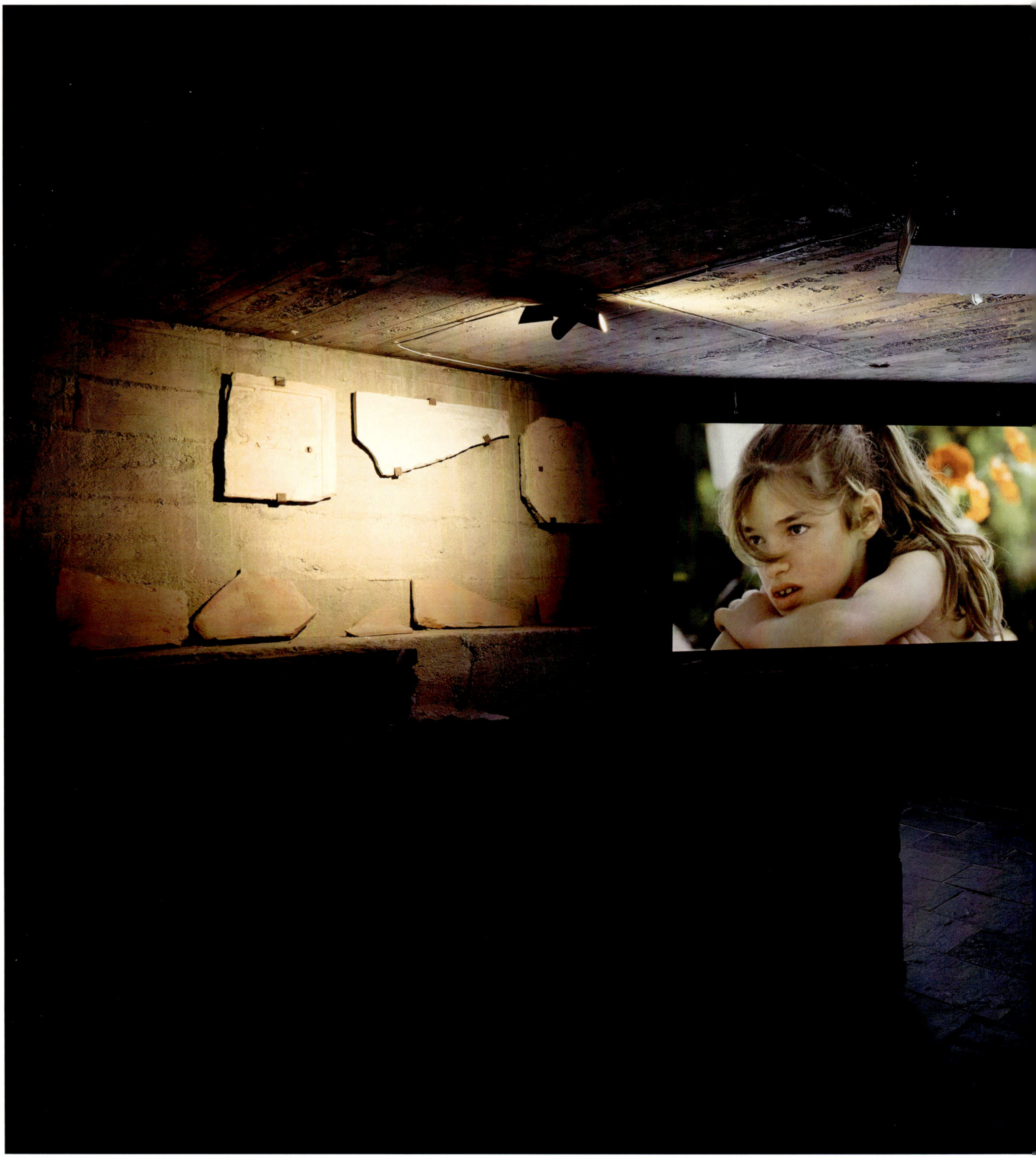

The Guardians, 2015
HD video, color, sound / Video HD, colore, suono, 6' 25"
Courtesy of the artist / dell'artista and / e kaufmann repetto, Milano / New York, and / e Peter Kilchmann, Zurich

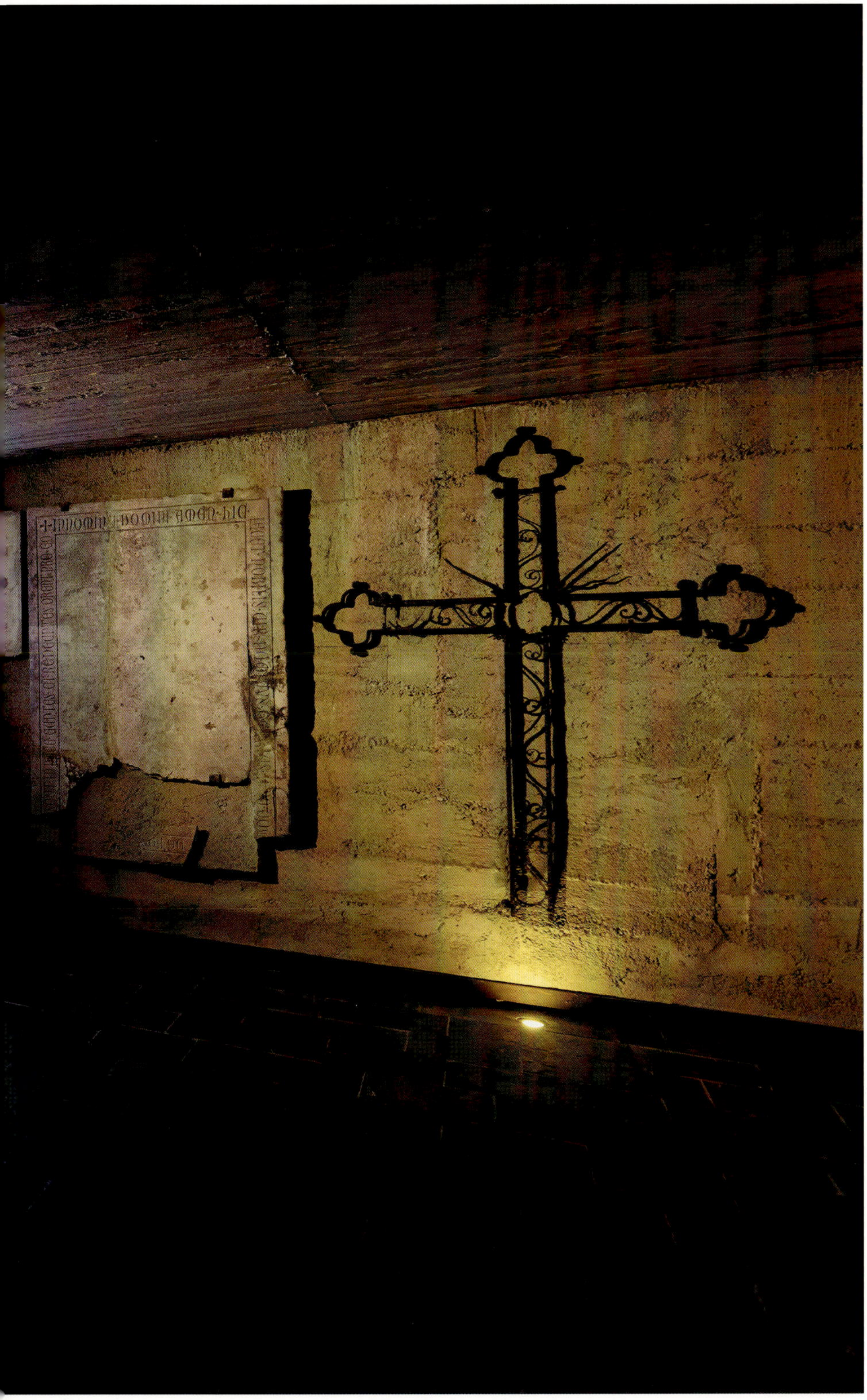

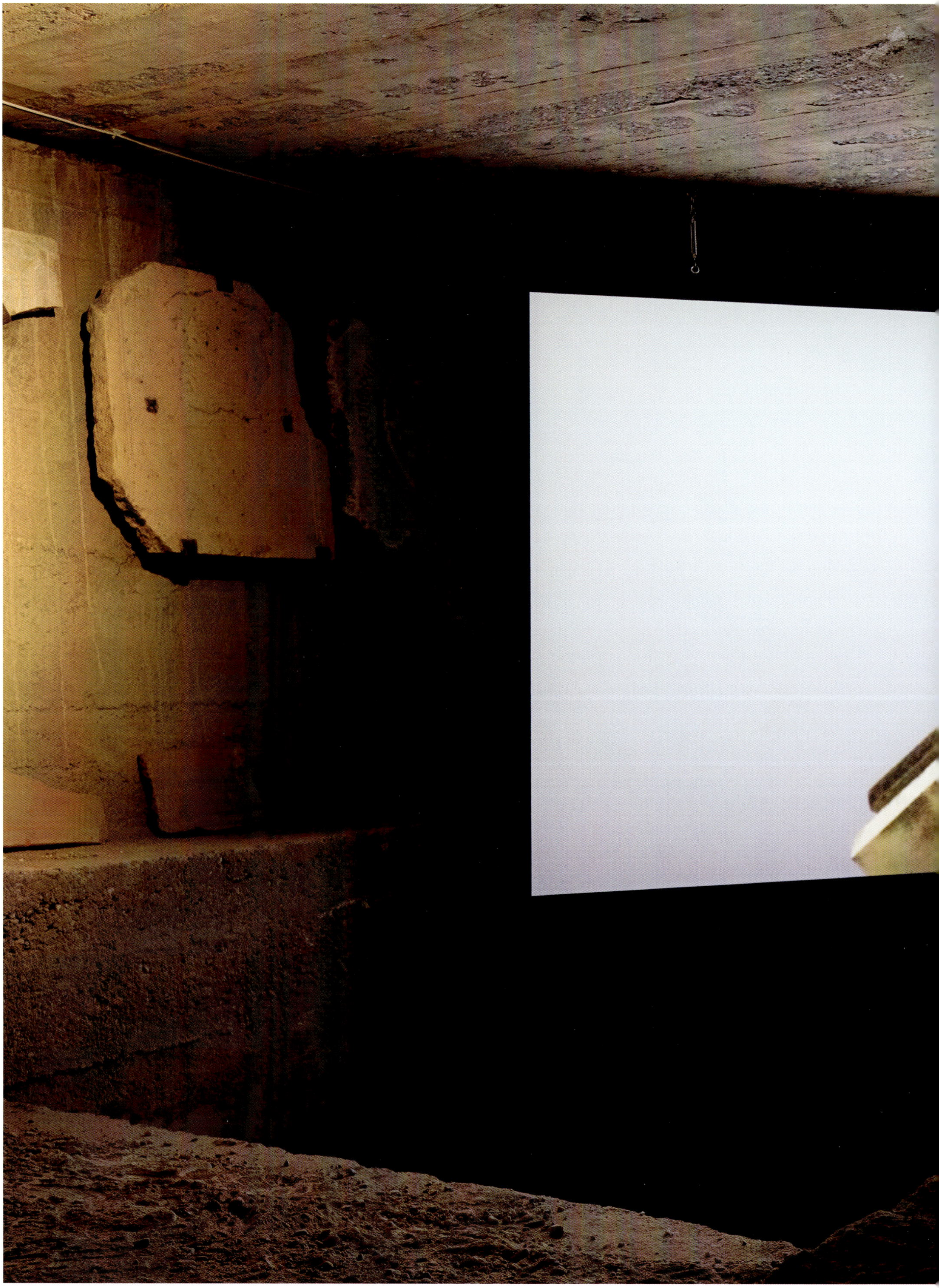

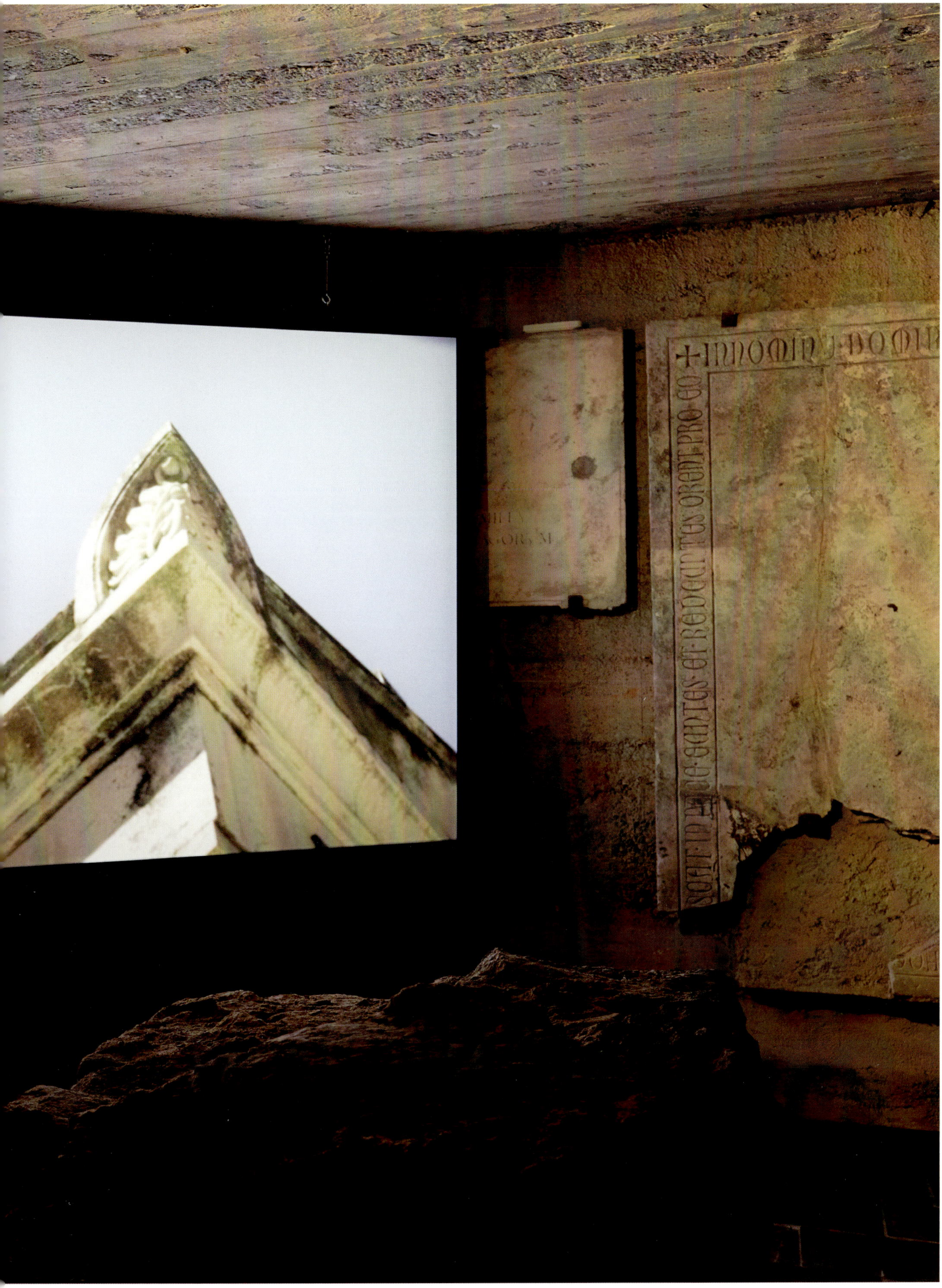

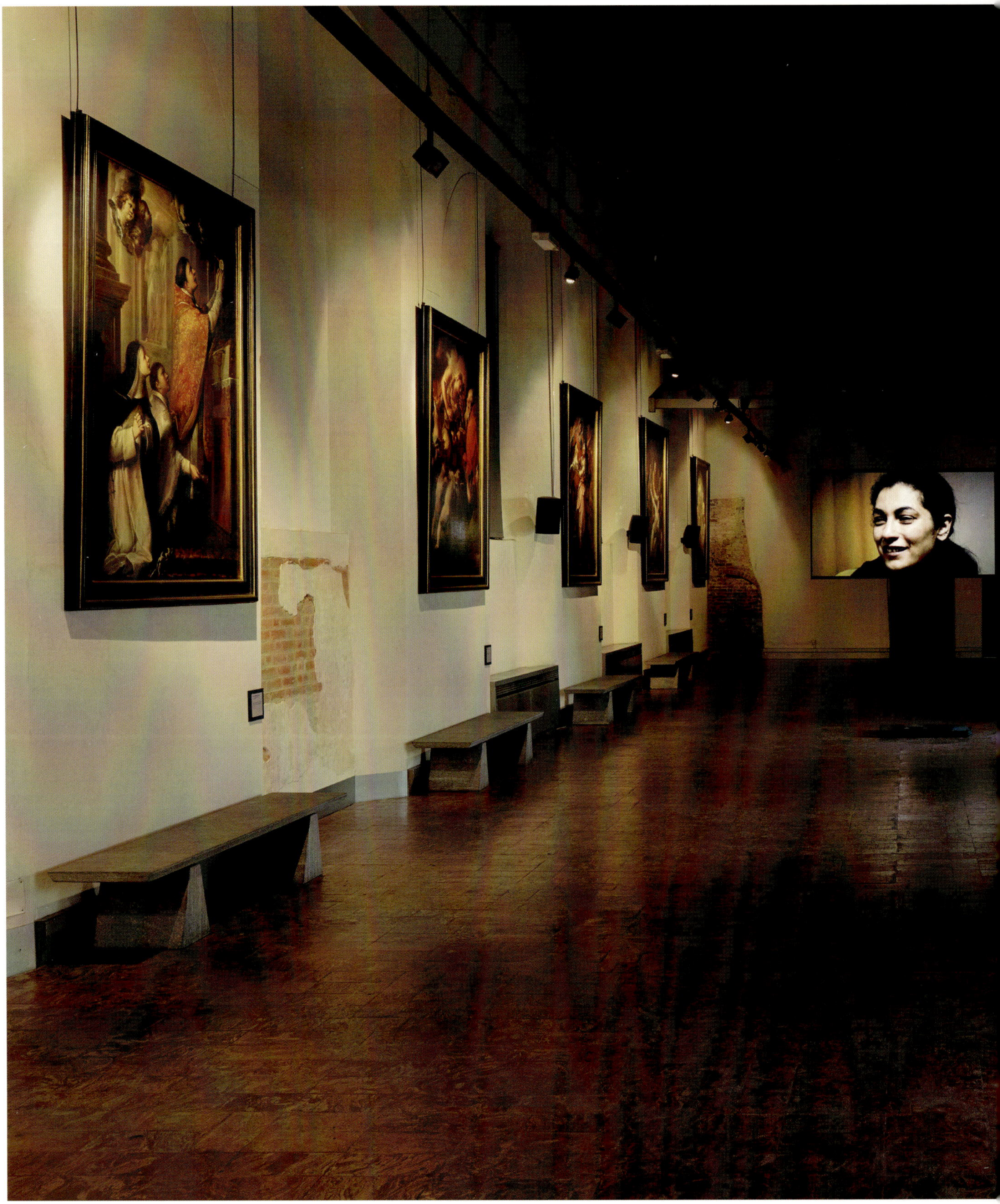

Rasha, 2017
Video, color, sound / Video, colore, suono, 20' 56"
Courtesy of the artist / dell'artista and / e kaufmann repetto, Milano / New York, and / e Peter Kilchmann, Zurich

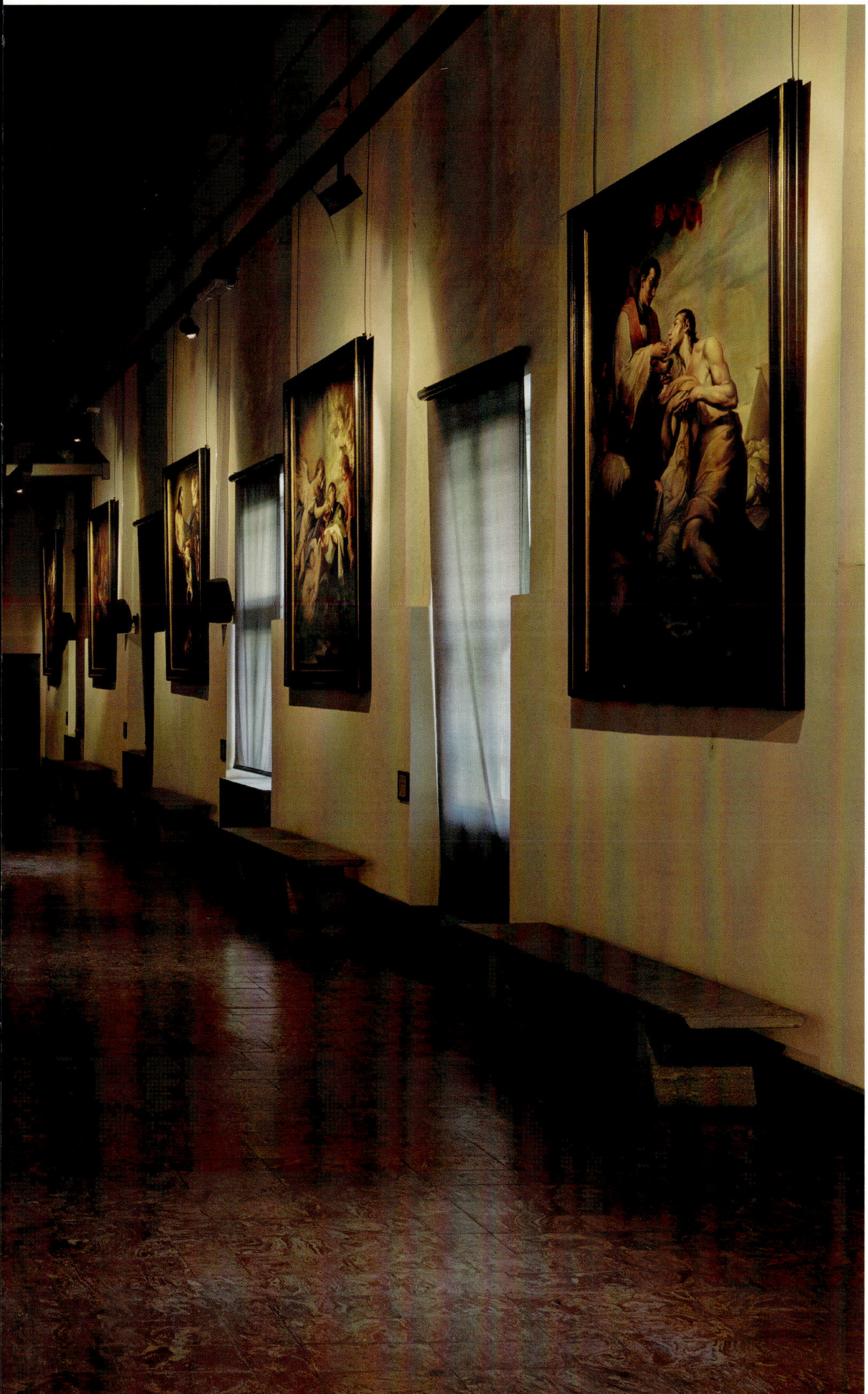

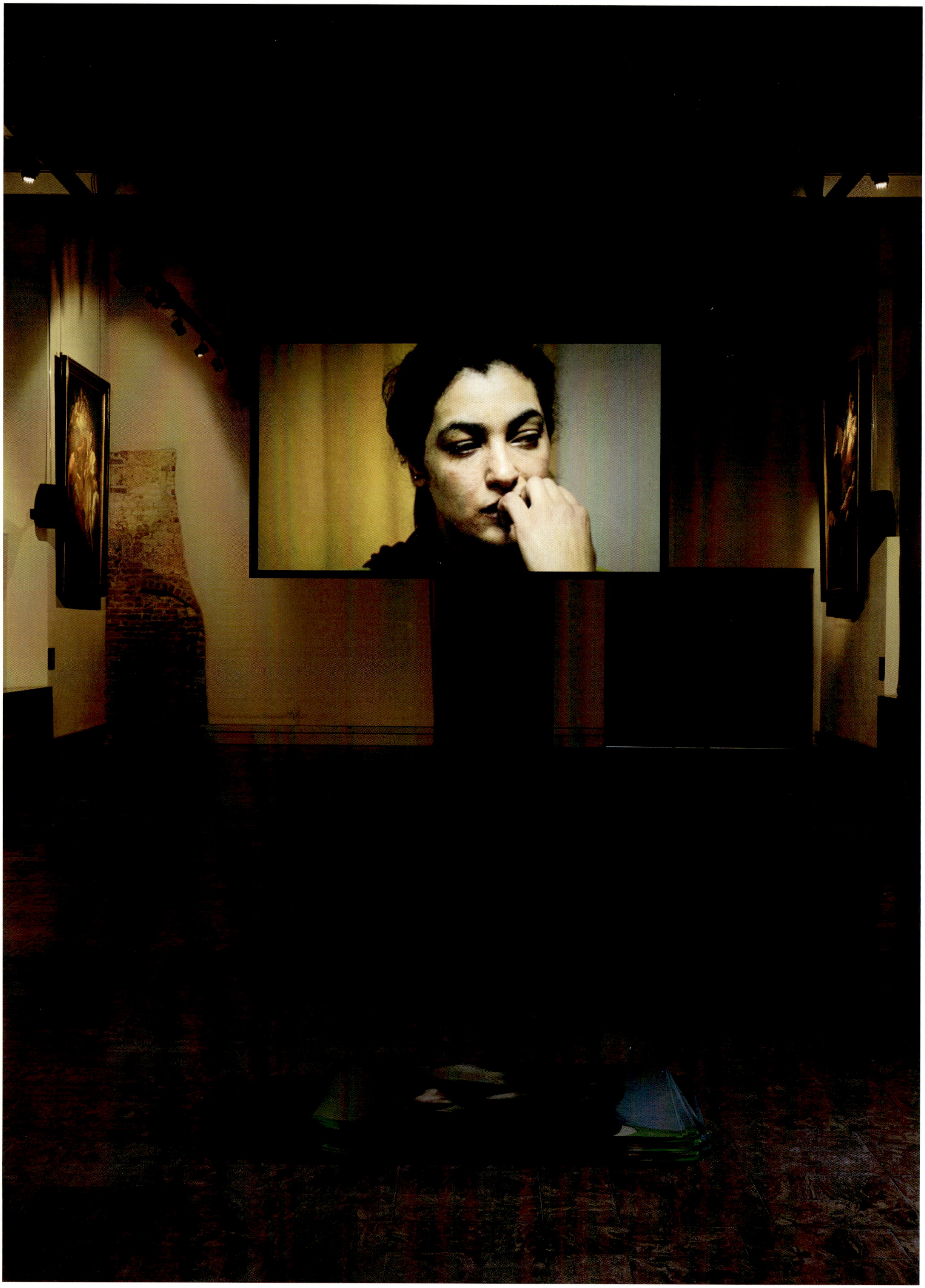

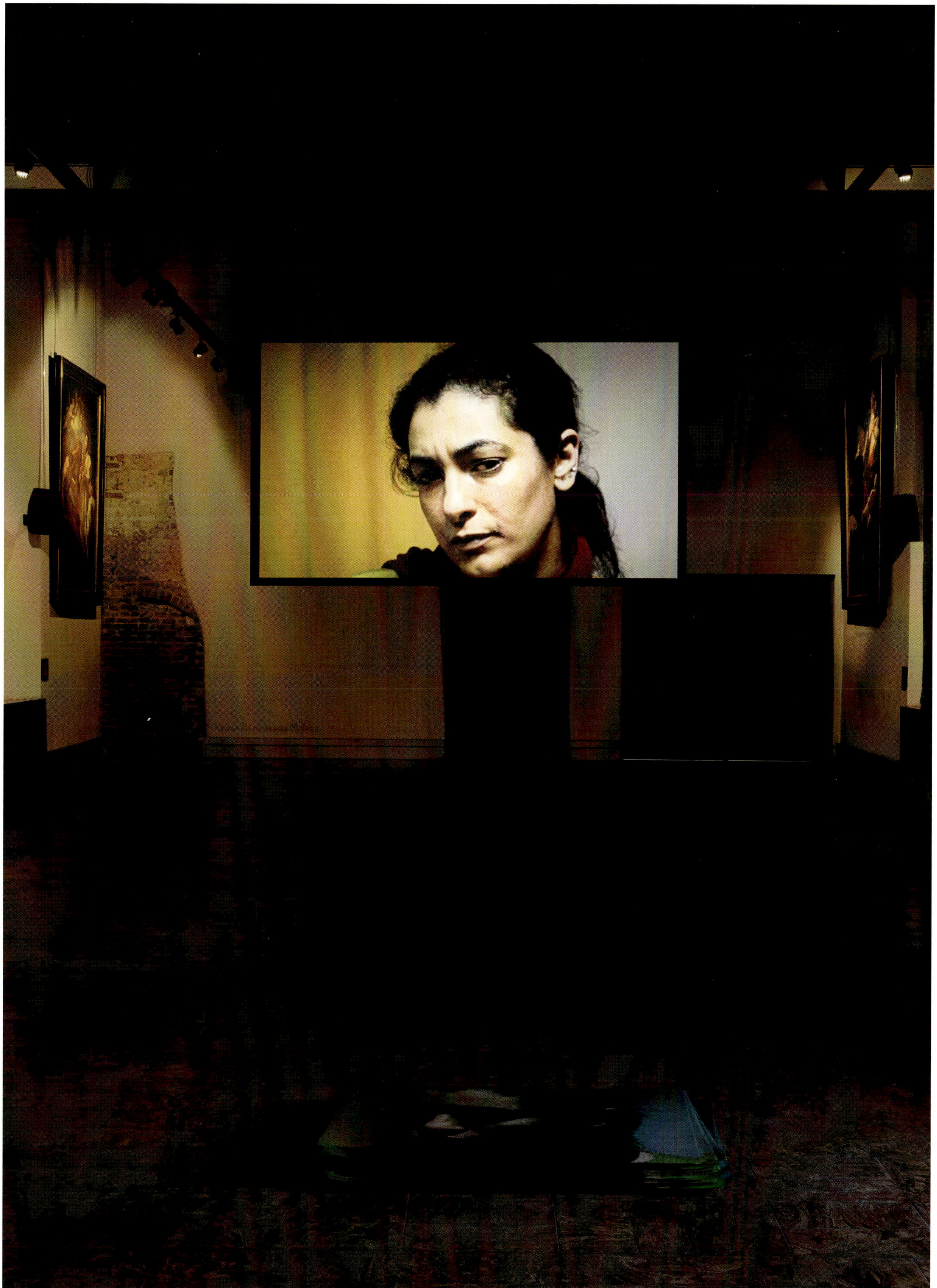

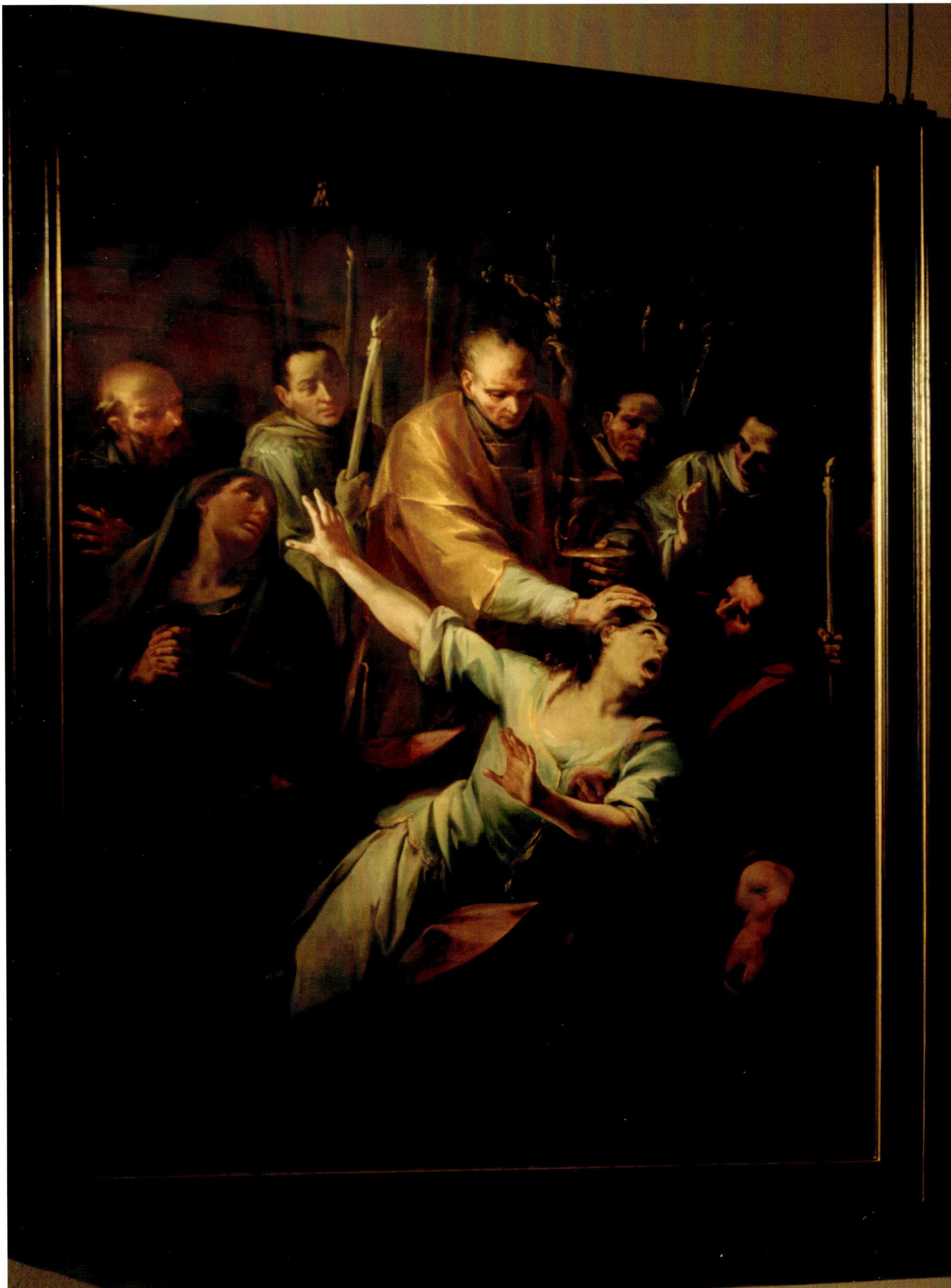

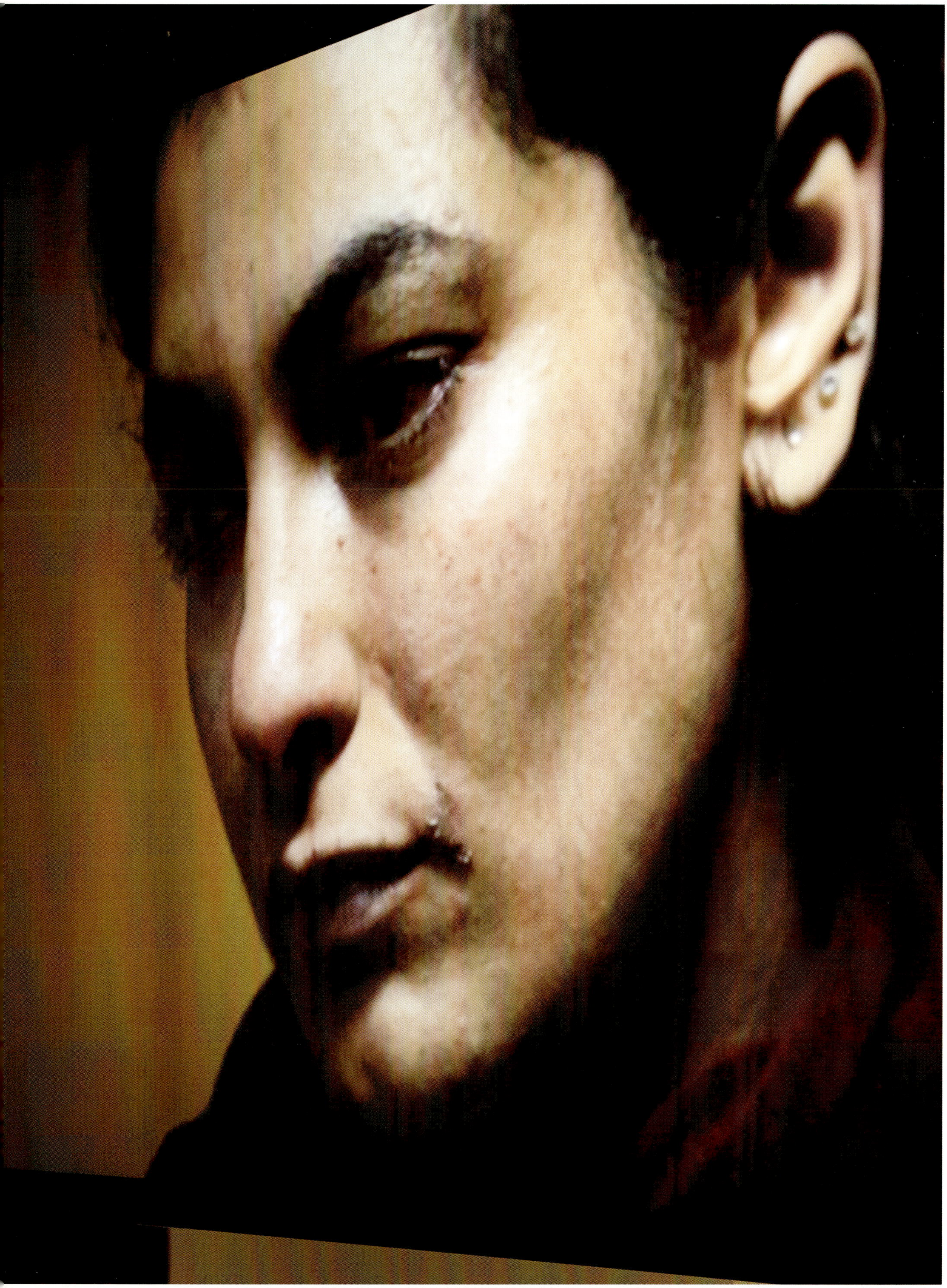

il presente, l'altrove, l'ulteriore

di gabi scardi

Per Adrian Paci l'arte si fa, di opera in opera, in un confronto continuo e mai definitivo con l'epoca presente e con il contesto, con la storia dell'arte e l'atto artistico stesso. Nel suo lavoro, che si nutre di una profonda familiarità con l'arte del passato, convivono l'osservazione delle dinamiche sociali del presente, l'attenzione per gesti che resistono ai cambiamenti di luogo e di tempo – e per questo acquistano densità iconica e di senso –, e un interesse per i significati sedimentati e per le possibilità interpretative dei segni e delle immagini.

Spazio di pensiero e conoscenza, di espressione e trasmissione di senso, ogni opera è basata, oltre che su una sensibilità immaginativa, sulla capacità di cogliere segnali esterni e interiori. Paci si muove con una chiarezza di idee e con una precisione dello sguardo che corrispondono a un atteggiamento etico. Il suo rapporto con la realtà è fatto di tensione, attenzione e rigore; di permeabilità e impegno; ma anche di singolarità e distanza; che sono una necessità e una forma di libertà.

Tra i motivi centrali delle sue opere ci sono il viaggio, l'attraversamento, l'attesa – che è, anzitutto, aspettativa di futuro – e il rapporto con il luogo e il tempo dell'origine, che non sono tanto dimensioni alle quali tornare, quanto riferimenti profondi da portare con sé. Questi temi vengono interpretati sulla base di una relazione attiva con la conoscenza, intesa come filtro attraverso il quale decodificare il mondo.

Albanese di nascita, italiano di adozione dal 1997, Adrian Paci è cresciuto nell'Albania di Enver Hoxha che, sigillata in se stessa, proclamava l'uomo nuovo come risultato perfetto dell'ideologia nazional-comunista. Negli anni Novanta, mentre il caos si impadroniva del paese, Paci si trasferiva in Italia scoprendo le contraddizioni di una società diversa, orientata anch'essa a generare un nuovo tipo di umanità: quella consumista, individualista, massificata e vieppiù globale dell'Occidente che conosciamo. Forse per questo le grandi dichiarazioni non gli sono proprie, le mode non lo impressionano, le posizioni astratte e universali gli ispirano diffidenza. D'altra parte, la contingenza non è sufficiente ad appagarlo. Ad attrarlo sono gesti ed espressioni magari quotidiani ma sobri e solenni insieme, capaci di farsi esemplari in virtù di una matrice antica e profonda. Oltrepassando i limiti dello spazio e del tempo, essi rendono tangibile un sostrato culturale che, come un minimo comune denominatore, avvicina gli uomini. Sono gesti, atti e atteggiamenti come una stretta di mano, che è il soggetto di *The Encounter* (2011); l'espressione tesa di una sposa che saluta i familiari da cui il matrimonio sta per separarla (*The Kiss*, 2008); il viso concentrato dei cavatori che, in *The Column* (2013), estraggono dalla montagna un grande blocco di marmo; o quello segnato degli uomini in attesa di intraprendere un viaggio verso una vita più accettabile in *The Line* (2007); o almeno di riuscire a trovare un datore di lavoro per la giornata, come in *Turn On* (2004).

Significativamente, la mostra *The Guardians* si apre con la sequenza fotografica *The Encounter*: il sagrato di una chiesa antica; al centro, un uomo in piedi scambia una stretta di mano con centinaia di persone che, abbigliate come in un giorno qualsiasi, verso di lui convergono non si sa da dove né perché, e poi proseguono, lasciandoselo alle spalle. La stretta di mano è consueta, semplice, concreta ma significativa: è scambio, patto, suggello, fratellanza. Nell'ambito di *The Encounter* accentuano il valore rituale sia il fatto che il tutto si svolga in questa area di rispetto tra il luogo sacro e la pubblica strada, sia la ripetizione che lo trasforma in una sorta di rito: la vita si sostanzia nell'autenticità con cui, quotidianamente, ci rivolgiamo all'altro che ci viene incontro; e questo incontro è, in se stesso, una cerimonia degna di essere celebrata ogni giorno.

L'attenzione a questi gesti densi non allontana Paci dalle vicende del mondo attuale; gli consente anzi di collocarle sullo sfondo di una storia antica e profonda per poterne meglio interpretare le dinamiche più specifiche e cogenti. La sua riflessione verte sul rapporto tra politica, economia e giustizia sociale, sulla crisi contemporanea della cittadinanza e, in particolare, sulle condizioni di coloro che sono spinti ad abbandonare la propria casa; sull'emigrazione, l'esilio, lo sradicamento. Lo colpiscono le situazioni di separatezza e di limbo di fuggiaschi e profughi, e la loro ricerca di asilo. Per Paci il migrante è una figura prossima. Lo si constata guardando *The Line* e i due video *Klodi* (2005) e *My Song in Your Kitchen* (2017).

Il primo è un dittico fotografico che presenta una fila di persone su una pista di decollo deserta; individui carichi di potenzialità, ma bloccati, isolati, in silenziosa attesa di un aereo che non c'è. Qui si intersecano diversi piani di riflessione: quello più universale, che vede l'uomo sempre in transito: è il senso di precarietà, l'idea di un "altrove" che ci accompagna sempre, è il viaggio improgrammabile dell'esistenza; l'altro, connesso con il fenomeno della migrazione, riguarda i molti che oggi sono costretti a intraprendere viaggi della speranza verso paesi diversi dal proprio; paesi che, in molti casi, si rivelano poco ospitali e li relegano in una difficile, quando non tragica, situazione di limbo. Nella sua apparente semplicità, l'immagine, come tutta la serie di opere a cui afferisce – comprendente, tra l'altro, l'ormai iconica opera *Centro di permanenza temporanea* (2007) –, si manifesta con una necessità e una compiutezza poetica che la rendono capace di generare momenti di contatto e risonanza profondi.

Klodi è il video-ritratto in presa diretta di un giovane uomo sempre in transito, perennemente alla ricerca di un futuro migliore, di lavoro, diritti, benessere, o semplicemente della possibilità di sopravvivere. In un mondo in cui l'identità è definita e controllata dalle politiche nazionali, tuttavia, non gli è dato poter riformulare se stesso, né recuperare legami sociali. Klodi rappresenta lo sradicato per eccellenza: separato dai luoghi e dalle persone, clandestino e senza protezione, continuamente costretto alla fuga. La possibilità di "fare casa" risulta per lui, con lo spiraliforme procedere della storia, sempre più irrealizzabile. L'uomo finisce per vivere una situazione drammatica e assurda, di alienazione e periplo permanente, la cui conclusione è ignota. Paci lo incontra e dedica il tempo necessario al racconto. Mentre ascoltiamo la sua voce, sullo schermo compaiono le traiettorie, tratteggiate a mano, lungo le quali Klodi ha transitato attraverso l'Europa: è la geografia alternativa di una persona ridotta a una vita precaria e senza stato. Ma a restare impresso è il racconto, sottratto al silenzio, e l'espressione inquieta ma vitale del suo viso, sottratto all'opacità e riportato per una volta in primo piano.

My Song in Your Kitchen è invece un video realizzato a Milano, all'interno di Casa Monluè: un centro che ospita temporaneamente i titolari di protezione internazionale. Si tratta di spazi vibranti di umanità, nostalgia, aspirazione verso il futuro. Qui Paci ha istituito una correlazione tra il cibo e la musica, entrambi legati agli affetti e ai ricordi d'infanzia, alle relazioni più intime e basilari, agli usi quotidiani dei luoghi di origine; dimensioni entrambe vitali, condensati di storie e di memorie, veicoli di desiderio e di un senso di convivialità. Su invito dell'artista, infatti, le cucine impersonali e spaesanti di Casa Monluè sono state utilizzate per preparare cibi da condividere, cantando, trasformandosi in spazi di relazione. Nei gesti dei giovani uomini coinvolti, provenienti da diversi paesi del continente africano, nelle pietanze semplici e nelle mani che ripetono gesti di casa, nei suoni portati dai luoghi di provenienza emergono lacerti di vite passate. Paci ha anche innestato sulle immagini una musica albanese, suonata da un complesso italiano. In questo modo la cesura rispetto a loro si è attenuata, lasciando spazio a una forma di profonda – e in molti momenti gioiosa – compartecipazione. Ad aprire e chiudere il video restano i lunghi corridoi vuoti che, con tante porte chiuse sui lati, continuano a trasmettere un senso di transizione e di incognita.

La presenza di quest'opera realizzata all'interno di un luogo marginale – in ogni senso: sociale, geografico, mentale – nel magnifico spazio di Sant'Eustorgio non è fortuita; è invece un invito a riflettere sullo stato di urgenza e solitudine delle persone da poco approdate nel paese e, d'altra parte, sulle loro potenzialità, sul loro desiderio di collaborare e di gioire nella condivisione: sul diritto di tutti a esserci.

Un senso di intimità caratterizza tutta l'opera di Adrian Paci. È un'intimità che non comporta un ritiro dal mondo ma, anzi, un'attenzione dello sguardo; che non induce il contrarsi dell'esperienza ma una sua maggiore profondità. Svetlana Boym, nel suo libro *The Future of Nostalgia*, la chiama "intimità diasporica", interpretandola come una speciale forma di adesione che trova appiglio nell'esperienza personale;

"L'intimità diasporica", scrive Boym, "potrebbe essere vista come la reciproca attrazione tra due migranti di diverse parti del mondo o come il senso di precario calore di una casa estranea. Nel momento in cui si impara a vivere con l'alienazione e ci si riconcilia con l'incomprensibilità del mondo circostante e l'estraneità del contatto umano, sopraggiunge una sorpresa, un brivido di intimo riconoscimento, una speranza che si insinua dalla porta posteriore nella nebbia dell'abituale straniamento della vita quotidiana all'estero".[1]

In Paci, questa forma di vicinanza che ha origine in una relazione tra biografia individuale e collettiva, oltrepassa ampiamente l'esperienza personale, innescando interrogativi di ordine etico, estetico e politico. Di più: muovendosi nel punto in cui piani diversi s'intersecano, Paci vede nella migraticità non solo l'intera storia dell'uomo ma la condizione più propria dell'artista e un continuo stimolo a immaginare nuovi modi di vivere, nuove possibili relazioni con il contesto, nuovi linguaggi con i quali esprimersi.

Esemplare della sua capacità di istituire una relazione tra biografia individuale e memoria condivisa, con il corpo del singolo che si fa collettivo e finisce per rappresentare un archetipo, è *Home to Go*: una scultura in cui l'artista si ritrae a grandezza naturale, spogliato di tutto, in cammino con il tetto di una casa sulle spalle. La scultura risale al 2001; negli stessi anni, Paci elaborava un nucleo di lavoro legato al tema del distacco e della perdita di cui fanno parte *Back Home* (2001) e *Vajtojca* (2002). Ma qui la sintesi e l'espansione simbolica raggiungono il massimo.

Illuminata, solitaria al centro della Sacrestia Monumentale di Sant'Eustorgio, la figura funge da testimonianza e monumento insieme, e costituisce un'espressione eloquente della fatica di avanzare carichi di passato e del pesante fardello rappresentato da un'identità stratificata. Conciliare il senso di appartenenza con la realtà della dislocazione è un'esperienza complessa, che comporta una cesura profonda. La vita stessa è interpretata come fatica e passione. Ma oltre il lutto, sembra dire l'opera, è possibile riprendere il cammino.

Home to Go pone al centro l'uomo, il viandante, il pellegrino e rammenta a chi la guarda che siamo tutti unici e importanti; e tutti stranieri, sempre in cammino sulla scena del mondo. L'opera, inoltre, risuona, rispetto all'ambiente impregnato di sacralità che la circonda, tra gli oggetti liturgici e i reliquiari, ed evoca con grande forza di suggestione

1 "Diasporic Intimacy could be seen as the mutual attraction of two immigrants from different parts of the world or the sense of a precarious coziness of a foreign home. Just as one learns to live with alienation and reconciles oneself to the uncanniness of the surrounding world and to the strangeness of the human touch, there comes a surprise, a pang of intimate recognition, a hope that sneaks in through the back door in the mist of the habitual estrangement of everyday life abroad." Svetlana Boym, *The Future of Nostalgia*, Basic Books, New York 2001. La traduzione in Italiano è a cura del traduttore.

una dimensione che eccede e trascende le azioni umane. Il tetto rovesciato richiama un paio di ali spiegate ad accogliere quanto potrà arrivare.

Se tutta l'opera di Paci è animata da una spiritualità primaria e rinvia a un destino che supera il caduco e l'effimero, in *Home to Go* il riferimento all'iconografia religiosa della Passione è evidente. Paci dedicherà al tema della Passione diverse opere, nell'arco di un decennio, come la *Cappella Pasolini* (2005) e la *Via Crucis* (2011) per la chiesa milanese di San Bartolomeo. Per l'artista, cresciuto in un'Albania chiusa non solo al mondo esterno ma a ogni esperienza di ulteriorità, l'idea di una dimensione religiosa e spirituale era sempre passata attraverso la lezione dei libri di arte antica lasciatigli dal padre Ferdinand Paci, a sua volta pittore: una lezione che aveva il senso di una scoperta, di un'esperienza e di una forma di educazione dello sguardo.

Profondamente assimilata, la conoscenza dell'arte classica emerge in tutta l'opera dell'artista e si declina di volta in volta in modi diversi. Tra le diverse possibilità che esplora c'è la rielaborazione di immagini antiche attraverso modalità moderne, e viceversa. È il caso di *Brothers* (2010). Nella Cappella Portinari, quest'opera a mosaico dialoga con gli affreschi rinascimentali di Vincenzo Foppa e con la monumentale Arca marmorea di San Pietro Martire scolpita da Giovanni di Balduccio. *Brothers* è giustapposta all'Arca e allineata sul medesimo asse visivo, quindi percepibile anche attraverso i suoi pilastri a colonna. Come le altre opere della serie "Passages", *Brothers* è realizzata a partire dal frammento di un filmato d'archivio, tra i tanti che l'artista colleziona: filmati spesso amatoriali, riferiti a cerimonie tradizionali o a momenti di vita comune, per lo più in Albania. In questo caso, nel *frame* estrapolato si coglie l'interazione fugace tra due fratelli; la microstoria, del tutto marginale, viene però riproposta attraverso una tecnica antica, altamente codificata, seppur oggi desueta; una tecnica che generalmente rende ardua l'espressione del dettaglio e che tende a congelare le immagini in una fissità ieratica.

In *Brothers* l'immagine si fa forte proprio delle caratteristiche tecniche e della matericità del mosaico per acquisire un senso di stabilità e di dilatazione temporale. Tuttavia, straordinariamente, non perde la connotazione dinamica del video, mantenendo invece la fugacità dell'istantanea e la mobilità della luce, ottenuta, quest'ultima, giocando non tanto sulla lucentezza delle tessere, come avviene tradizionalmente, ma su altezze e sporgenze irregolari che, realizzate a scalpello, contribuiscono a generare effetti di luce e ombra. Il tassellato di marmo e smalto evoca, inoltre, i pixel del video sgranato. Il risultato è un'immagine enigmatica, in cui i gesti semplici continuano a trasmettere un senso di intimità, acquisendo, al contempo, intensità e assolutezza. Così, grazie a un'analitica attenzione al dettaglio e a un'assoluta consapevolezza dei mezzi e del linguaggio dell'arte, Paci coniuga il tempo meditato ed elaborato del mosaico con la virtualità del video, attraverso la fisicità di una tecnica che viene rinnovata dall'interno.

Il lavoro nasce sia dall'interesse di Paci per le innumerevoli possibilità d'interpretazione di cui ogni immagine è portatrice, sia dalla convinzione che, della realtà che si presenta allo sguardo, tendiamo oggi a cogliere le medesime strutture visive sulle quali gli artisti di un tempo costruivano i propri dipinti. È Masaccio, in particolare, a emergere nella figura di Rasha, dal cui incontro nasce il video che porta il suo nome (*Rasha*, 2017). Paci ne rinviene la memoria durante la fase di montaggio dell'opera.

Rasha Meish è una donna palestinese, proveniente dalla Siria e approdata a Roma nel 2016 grazie ai corridoi umanitari. Nel video viene ripresa mentre, su sua richiesta, racconta la propria storia. Le immagini che scorrono, però, corrispondono ai momenti in cui, tra una frase e l'altra, la donna tace, in attesa che le sue parole vengano tradotte. La vediamo ascoltare in silenzio la propria storia. La sua presenza fisica è forte. La postura, i gesti, le espressioni che si alternano sul suo volto comunicano non solo la tensione del racconto interrotto per un attimo appena, ma tutta la forza di un'esperienza vissuta; un'esperienza che, malgrado lo sforzo di esprimere l'essenziale, non è del tutto parafrasabile a parole.

Come evidenzia Paci, tra la narrazione verbale e quella del corpo, tra il volto silenzioso e la voce che racconta in Arabo, si crea una sfasatura: Rasha diventa la protagonista non solo della storia, ma anche dell'ascolto. A parte, su un foglio che è possibile portare via con sé, si ritrovano, tradotte, le sue parole; necessarie, ma non sufficienti. L'opera costituisce una riflessione sulle tracce che il passato lascia sui nostri corpi e su come il corpo stesso le trasmetta. Le sfaccettature dell'espressione del volto della donna comunicano al di là delle parole. *Rasha* è un'opera sulla complessità della testimonianza e su come un racconto si faccia non solo attraverso la parola ma anche attraverso il linguaggio del corpo. La sua è una storia di violenza, di separazione dai luoghi e dagli affetti; è la storia di un trauma, ma anche di un riscatto possibile grazie alla solidarietà e all'amicizia. È importante conoscerla, perché in filigrana vi si legge il dolore di innumerevoli persone. Per questo Paci indugia, come in altre opere, sul suo volto. Un'attenzione che non nasce da un'attitudine descrittiva ma diviene atto di rispetto per l'individuo; per ogni individuo. Da qui lo slittamento dal piano della contingenza a quello del simbolo.

Nell'odierno sovraffollato universo visivo, tra le innumerevoli immagini che si accavallano, il volto di Rasha emerge e si staglia vivido e chiaro. Così, con lo sguardo posato sulle immagini, da un lato, un'attenzione vigile sulla realtà, dall'altro, e l'esercizio di un'immaginazione sempre mobile, Paci interroga l'opera nel suo farsi. Questo processo funge da filtro e implica una distanza che gli consente, una volta di più, di raccontare un'epoca e le sue contraddizioni, trasformando una vicenda individuale in una storia che ne ingloba infinite altre.

Nella Sala dell'Arciconfraternita in cui è esposta, *Rasha* si inserisce in un racconto corale; il video, infatti, è collocato al centro di un ciclo di quadri devozionali settecenteschi di grandi dimensioni dall'andamento narrativo. L'allestimento evoca il significato narrativo dei grandi cicli pittorici del passato ma fa anche pensare a una teoria cinematografica fatta di *frame*. L'espressività mobile e sensibile di Rasha dialoga con la gestualità enfatica e teatrale dei personaggi dipinti, con la meccanica della macchina fotografica che sostituisce la manualità della pittura, e un primissimo piano orizzontale a ripresa fissa, tipicamente cinematografico, alla movimentata scenografia teatrale circoscritta da quinte che si trova nei quadri. L'avvicendarsi dei mezzi e delle modalità ha a che fare con un passaggio d'epoca ormai avvenuto. Pur così diverse, tuttavia, le figure sono accomunate dall'emotività che le anima, resa in entrambi i casi evidente da un'accentuata illuminazione.

Anche *Malgrado tutto* (2017) evoca l'inestinguibile necessità umana di espressione. Si tratta di una serie di fotografie dei graffiti tuttora visibili sulle pareti scabre delle celle di un antico monastero francescano che, durante la dittatura comunista di Enver Hoxha, funse da prigione. Qui, dalla fine della Seconda guerra mondiale fino agli anni Novanta, i prigionieri albanesi venivano rinchiusi, interrogati e torturati. In parte reintegrato nella funzione originaria di monastero, in parte trasformato in Museo della Memoria, il luogo conserva ancora i segni delle loro sofferenze, vissute nel silenzio: disegni, parole, calendari incisi sui muri per segnare il tempo. Sono testimonianze ormai labili, ma intense, del bisogno dell'uomo di lasciare traccia del proprio vissuto, sinanco nelle condizioni di privazione estrema. L'artista le coglie e le fissa fotograficamente prima che scompaiano, mettendo così in campo un commento sul proprio paese e sulle sue trasformazioni, per poi allargare la riflessione ai grandi temi del tempo, della memoria e dell'oblio.

Ancora una volta, l'opera prende forma attraverso uno slittamento tra diverse modalità di espressione. La ricerca di Paci si sviluppa nel confronto con i linguaggi che continuamente convivono e si intersecano nel mondo, e che sono solo in parte traducibili gli uni negli altri. Proprio facendo appello a questa complessità linguistica si può esprimere la ricchezza dell'esistente.

Malgrado tutto ha trovato spazio sui muri del cimitero paleocristiano di Sant'Eustorgio. I segni fragili ma resistenti del recente passato albanese si confrontano con steli ed epigrafi emerse nel corso dei ritrovamenti archeologici; e in questo ambiente risuonano con potenza, testimoniando della capacità umana di lasciare segni che fungono da ponte attraverso il tempo.

Nello stesso ambiente si vede *The Guardians* (2015): il video racconta del cimitero cattolico di Scutari dismesso durante la dittatura. Divenuto sede di incontri altrimenti impossibili, recuperato nel 1991 in seguito alla caduta del regime, da quel momento il luogo viene investito da un fenomeno di proliferazione entusiasta ma disordinata, ed è oggi animato da bambini che si fanno pagare per prendersi cura delle tombe: un fenomeno che rispecchia la contraddittoria ma inarrestabile rinascita del paese.

La disinvoltura dei bambini testimonia, inoltre, le innumerevoli sfaccettature possibili nella nostra relazione con la vita e con la morte; l'energia che profondono dice la forza di libertà che spinge l'uomo a infrangere costrizioni e barriere; il loro impegno li connota come guardiani del futuro. Il cimitero paleocristiano, in cui la morte è presente, è pur sempre un luogo di vita. E anche la riflessione sull'aldilà può essere un'occasione per meglio operare qui. Quest'opera, che vibra di tensione poetica e di vitalità, parla con leggerezza di una necessaria premura per l'esistente, delle giovani generazioni che si affacciano, del nuovo che erompe ma anche della possibilità di creare una comunione reale, intima, concreta con il passato; di istituire una cinghia di trasmissione affinché ciò che ha valore possa restare patrimonio comune per chi verrà.

L'opera di Paci nasce da una profonda fiducia nell'arte e nelle sue capacità di aprire spazi di riflessione. La giustezza del suo sguardo, la precisa definizione dei dettagli, gli intensi primi piani ricorrenti evidenziano come la contingenza non ne sia espunta, ma sottoposta a un filtro che la condensa fino all'essenziale. In questa sintesi, a ogni opera si rinnova il cortocircuito tra la dimensione più arcaica e profonda, persistente negli atteggiamenti umani e sedimentata nelle immagini che la storia dell'arte ci ha lasciato; e quella del presente più cogente, in cui le dinamiche geopolitiche hanno drastiche ripercussioni sulle vite dei singoli. Il senso della sua opera scaturisce da questa coesistenza di circostanza e universalità, di compartecipazione e distanza, di poesia e critica: una critica che si fa continua asserzione del valore fondamentale della dignità, che non può che essere soggettiva e collettiva, morale e sociale al contempo. Paci si inserisce così pienamente nel discorso pubblico riguardante i fondamenti del rispetto, della giustizia e della convivenza.

disconnettere e triangolare

di charles esche

Se non possiamo indovinare come diventerà il mondo, possiamo almeno immaginare come ci piacerebbe vederlo diventare. Il diritto a sognare non figurava nella Dichiarazione universale dei diritti dell'uomo proclamata dalle Nazioni Unite alla fine del 1948. Ma senza di esso, senza il diritto a sognare e le acque con cui li abbevera, gli altri diritti moriranno di sete.
Eduardo Galeano[1]

Lo scrittore e giornalista uruguaiano Eduardo Galeano conosceva bene il potere della sofferenza. Da esule, vide il suo maltrattato continente languire sotto lo stivale dei dittatori per buona parte del ventesimo secolo. Eppure i suoi scritti non smisero mai di evocare la possibilità di emancipazione che si cela sotto il dolore. La sua rassegnazione era sempre contaminata dalla possibilità che le cose prima o poi prendessero un'altra piega. Sembra pertinente citare lo scrittore Galeano in relazione alla mostra che Adrian Paci ha allestito nella chiesa milanese di Sant'Eustorgio, perché anche questa gioca, in tanti modi diversi, con l'equilibrio tra sofferenza e liberazione, riflettendo il potere simbolico della sofferenza e il modo in cui questo può essere usato per trasformare o trascendere la causa immediata del malessere.

Il lavoro centrale della mostra, o almeno quello che mi sembra fare da punto di partenza, si intitola *Rasha* (2017): una monumentale immagine su schermo di una donna siriana accompagnata da una voce in arabo. Non è la donna, Rasha, a parlare; come noi, anche lei ascolta la sua stessa voce disincarnata. Di volta in volta annuisce nervosa, sorride, o appare confusa dalla storia che viene raccontata. Non comprendendo l'Arabo, mi sento costretto a guardare con attenzione il suo viso: ha un occhio appannato, forse conseguenza di qualche precedente violenza; l'altro sprizza una certa tensione. Il collo è rigido; spesso abbassa o distoglie lo sguardo, isolandosi nei suoi pensieri. L'effetto è ancora più forte in quanto ci troviamo nel refettorio domenicano della basilica, circondati da dipinti a olio del cattolicesimo romano – rappresentazioni un po' generiche del mito cristiano, tra cui una quantità di immagini frontali di Maria, madre di Gesù. Spostando lo sguardo dai quadri allo schermo, è difficile non ammettere che la Maria cristiana poteva essere descritta come una donna sofferente della stessa provenienza dell'altra.

Questa coincidenza di volti silenziosi e dolenti, separati nel tempo da due migliaia di anni, stanno a fondamento delle aspettative e

1 Eduardo Galeano da una conferenza sul diritto di sognare, https://www.youtube.com/watch?v=T1XqTBNxLys.
Tutte le traduzioni in Italiano sono a cura del traduttore.

potenzialità dell'intera mostra, allestita e concepita per uno spazio che è tanto un museo quanto un tempio cristiano. La Basilica di Sant'Eustorgio è il più antico edificio cristiano di Milano e, per un certo tempo, ha custodito le reliquie dei Re Magi. Rappresenta ancora oggi una importane tappa di pellegrinaggio sulla strada verso Roma. È dunque un contenitore particolarmente significativo per il lavoro di un artista di origine albanese, che ha completato la sua formazione artistica in una società ufficialmente atea che rifiutava il cristianesimo, l'islamismo e la modernità, ma ha finito per crollare sotto le sue stesse contraddizioni, e dunque ha smesso di rappresentare una posizione che l'artista deve difendere o contrastare come condizione a priori della sua pratica.

L'indipendenza sia dalla religione sia dall'ideologia garantita da questa insolita ambientazione crea una possibilità alternativa in una situazione inequivocabilmente cristiana. In particolare, permette alle intenzioni connaturate ai lavori di uscire dai parametri noti attraverso cui arte e religione solitamente si relazionano. Le immagini artistiche, basate sulla biografia del loro autore, non devono sobbarcarsi l'onere di illustrare una storia canonica o affermare una dottrina di fede; e nemmeno sono costrette a rifiutare i fondamenti di quella fede per poter plasmare il proprio discorso. La distanza di Paci dalla religione, insieme al fallimento del suo ateismo dogmatico d'origine, gli dà la possibilità di esporre in questa chiesa senza il peso di competere con essa, restando fedele alla sua ambivalenza rispetto al credo – religioso o modernista che sia. Se dovessimo inserire la mostra nel pensiero decoloniale, secondo me fondamentale per comprendere il mondo di oggi, potremmo considerarla un momento esemplare di disconnessione, in cui le linee predeterminate di connessione tra fenomeni materiali e immateriali vengono interrotte – o almeno molto allentate – per consentire il formarsi (o il riconnettersi, direbbe la teoria decoloniale) di nuovi rapporti.

Per chiarire il concetto, queste sono le parole di Walter Mignolo, uno dei principali teorici della decolonizzazione:

> *La società politica globale si è organizzata in una miriade di modi disparati, perché né lo Stato né il Mercato se ne è preoccupato. Qui svolge un ruolo fondamentale la rielaborazione della spiritualità. Sappiamo che la religione ha molti volti, e adesso non voglio addentrarmi nell'argomento, ma solo accennare al fatto che settori significativi delle religioni, di diverse religioni in diverse parti del mondo, stanno entrando nella società politica senza abbandonare le loro basi religiose. Uno dei compiti è decolonizzare la religione in modo da liberare la spiritualità.*[2]

In questi termini, collocare Rasha accanto a Maria è proprio uno di questi atti di decolonizzazione della religione. Entrambe le donne, forti, aggraziate, vulnerabili e misteriose, si trovano così potenzialmente liberate dai pregiudizi che le imprigionano – la "Madre di Dio" quanto la "profuga siriana" – per tornare a essere creature politiche e spirituali.

Questa strategia di incorporare l'ambiente della chiesa al fine di disconnettere sia il lavoro che la circostante architettura ecclesiastica dal suo contesto familiare è più volte rivisitata nella mostra. Il ripetersi della struttura di disconnessione e riconnessione non solo conferma la sua efficacia, ma permette a un terzo elemento più materialista di entrare nell'equazione. La scultura *Home to Go* (2001) è collocata, a pavimento, di fronte a un crocifisso, sotto cui si ergono due statue di donatori, uno dei quali ha un modellino di chiesa nella mano. Nella scultura di Paci, la figura in scala reale raffigurante l'artista sopporta quello che sembra essere il peso schiacciante di un tetto di tegole rovesciato sulla schiena. Lavoro duro, sforzo e sacrificio sono qui rappresentati, sia nella figura di Cristo sulla croce, sia nell'artista che porta il tetto su di sé. Il riferimento alla storia evangelica di Gesù che porta la croce per le strade di Gerusalemme è evidente, ma la figura del donatore sullo sfondo suggerisce anche che forse il tetto avrebbe potuto offrire una protezione collettiva. Questo fitto dialogo tra gli elementi esistenti presenti nella chiesa e la nuova opera crea una rinnovata visibilità per i decori della basilica e attira l'attenzione su quello che altrimenti sarebbe potuto apparire irrilevante, o una prevedibile conferma della tipica retorica cristiana, dato il suo collocamento in un luogo di culto cattolico.

Altri elementi costruiscono un processo altrettanto complesso di disconnessione e riconnessione nella modalità di quello che si stabilisce fra Rasha e Maria. Attorno al suddetto crocifisso si trova una serie di teche fastosamente allestite che mostrano i tesori in argento della chiesa con le loro dediche individuali a Dio e ai Suoi servitori. Come sfondo della rappresentazione di povertà redentrice della figura di Cristo e della scultura di Paci, queste teche suggeriscono una catena di associazioni il cui unico argomento possibile sono le attrattive di e le contraddizioni tra benessere materiale e purezza spirituale. Sia il corpo sul crocifisso che la figura che porta il tetto sono vestiti di stracci. La ricchezza dell'ambiente stride tanto più con questi corpi sofferenti, puntando l'attenzione sul lavoro non retribuito in diretto contrasto con il lusso degli accessori della chiesa romana.[3] Se ricordiamo di nuovo l'educazione socialista di Paci in

2 Walter Mignolo in un'intervista con Christopher Mattison, *Critical Legal Thinking*, 2 maggio 2012, http://criticallegalthinking.com/2012/05/02/delinking-decoloniality-dewesternization-interview-with-walter-mignolo-part-ii/.

3 È allettante vedere in questo monastero domenicano la disputa molto cattolica tra questo ordine mendicante e i loro rivali francescani, con l'insistenza dei secondi sulla proprietà comune e la deprivazione privata.

Albania, possiamo vedere qui non solo la frattura tra spirituale e religioso, come è stata espressa da Mignolo, ma anche una terza interpretazione materialistica del modo in cui le azioni sociali e culturali sono determinate dalle effettive condizioni materiali. Come scrisse Karl Marx in *L'ideologia tedesca*: "La natura degli individui dipende dalle condizioni materiali che determinano la loro produzione."[4] Qui, tre ideologie in competizione vengono esposte davanti a noi in una configurazione spaziale triangolare che è ammirevole per come evita di prendere partito, almeno in modo manifesto, o quanto meno perché comprende che niente lì sarebbe stato meno persuasivo dell'ennesima esegesi didattica della morale buona e cattiva.

Altrove, i gesti di disconnessione si esprimono in modi ancora più complessi. Alcuni scavi condotti nel diciannovesimo secolo sotto la cripta della basilica hanno rivelato un luogo di sepoltura cristiano del terzo o quarto secolo che oggi è aperto al pubblico. Le iscrizioni sulle tombe rivelano in parte una fede clandestina e perseguitata, per cui i suoi seguaci si sacrificavano. Al centro di questo cimitero artificialmente mantenuto, Paci ha collocato un cortometraggio che ha per protagonisti alcuni bambini della sua città natale, Shkoder, ripresi mentre si aggirano in un cimitero cristiano abbandonato. I paralleli letterali sono evidenti; tuttavia, questo lavoro non si limita a parlare di persecuzione cristiana e delle finzioni dell'archeologia, ma allude al culto della morte in quanto parte essenziale del cristianesimo. Mentre il film procede, vediamo sempre più bambini intenti a lavare le tombe, in quello che assomiglia a un rituale collettivo di purificazione, e in questo contesto non è difficile leggerlo come un'espiazione dei propri peccati. Forse ci troviamo di fronte a una spontanea reinumazione alla luce del fatto che oggi gli albanesi hanno il permesso di venerare i loro dei in pubblico. Ad aumentare la sensazione di riparare un torto, o riconnettere passato e presente, veniamo informati che, durante il regime comunista, questo cimitero è stato abbandonato per un lungo periodo e solo di recente ha riacquistato uno status ufficiale.

Altri due lavori della mostra (non in video) inseriscono un elemento supplementare alla disconnessione triangolata in cui religione, spiritualità e materialismo si riconfigurano gli uni attorno agli altri, aggiungendovi, in modo ancora più chiaro, il tempo e la storia. Il primo è una serie di fotografie intitolata *The Encounter* (2011) e realizzata in uno spazio difficilmente definibile, davanti a una chiesa barocca, nella città siciliana di Scicli. Si vede l'artista in piedi, vicino a una sedia, stringere la mano uno a uno agli abitanti del paese che formano una lunghissima fila attorno

4 "The nature of individuals thus depends on the material conditions determining their production". Karl Marx, *L'ideologia tedesca*, capitolo 1A, originalmente pubblicato nel 1845, https://www.marxists.org/archive/marx/works/1845/german-ideology/ch01a.htm.

alla piazza. Questo gesto dello straniero-artista che saluta è già di per sé interessante. L'associare un luogo specifico ai pregiudizi sui siciliani che li vorrebbero chiusi e omertosi, oltre alla splendida scenografia decadente dell'ambiente urbano mediterraneo, fa sì che la sequenza di fotografie si fondi su una triangolazione di luogo, storia e contemporaneità, all'interno di un contesto che, a prima vista, appare immutato e per secoli immutabile. Il sospetto è che qui ci sia la volontà di evocare fantasmi storici, nel senso che spesso la Sicilia viene raffigurata come soggetta a potenti forze esterne contro cui la mafia e la chiesa cattolica fungono da indispensabili scudi. Da questo punto di vista, potremmo avere qualche sospetto sulla genuinità dello scambio, o quanto meno sugli aspetti di pubblico rituale e dell'importanza di essere visti mentre si fa qualcosa rispetto al farlo e basta. Al tempo stesso, il rituale di benvenuto può essere interpretato come un modo di aprirsi ai nuovi arrivati e di introdurre una nuova forma di liturgia nel processo molto attuale di spaesamento e migrazione. Naturalmente nello spazio della chiesa milanese di Sant'Eustorgio permangono altri echi della storia interna italiana, tra occupazione settentrionale e resistenza meridionale.

L'ultimo lavoro di cui vorrei parlare si intitola *Brothers* (2010) ed è forse, dell'intera mostra, il più quotidiano. Un mosaico incorniciato in scala di grigi esposto in verticale sul pavimento, come uno schermo da proiezione, si trasforma, alla giusta distanza, nell'immagine di due ragazzini seduti uno accanto all'altro in un anonimo paesaggio rurale. I ragazzini hanno lo sguardo fisso fuori dall'immagine – i loro occhi sono alcune delle pietre più scure. Collocato davanti a un'elaborata cancellata di ferro, il mosaico richiama le forme bizantine di un'immagine ecclesiastica, spiccando così tra i quadri e le sculture che lo circondano. Inevitabilmente fa sì che l'immagine risulti monumentale usando un medium che difficilmente può essere letto se non in chiave simbolica o metaforica. Ci si trova poi davanti a un enigma. L'uso della scala di grigi richiama subito alla mente la fotografia in bianco e nero, evocando dunque un determinato periodo – la fine del diciannovesimo secolo o all'inizio del ventesimo –, mentre la tecnica può alludere a un tempo molto precedente o molto successivo. Nei volti frammentari dei due bambini è difficile non vedere un riflesso dei crimini contro l'umanità che hanno costellato gli ultimi cent'anni. Sapere che l'immagine può forse avere una fonte molto più innocente, per esempio un matrimonio di campagna, mette alla prova il senso di inquietudine, senza tuttavia eliminarlo. Come la spiritualità e la materialità dei primi lavori, *Brothers* porta tutto questo e ancora di più all'interno dell'immagine. Il diritto di sognare di Galeano non risolve nessuno di questi dilemmi esistenziali ma, come succede per l'acqua, senza di esso (senza quest'arte) gli esseri umani non avrebbero una vita degna di questo nome.

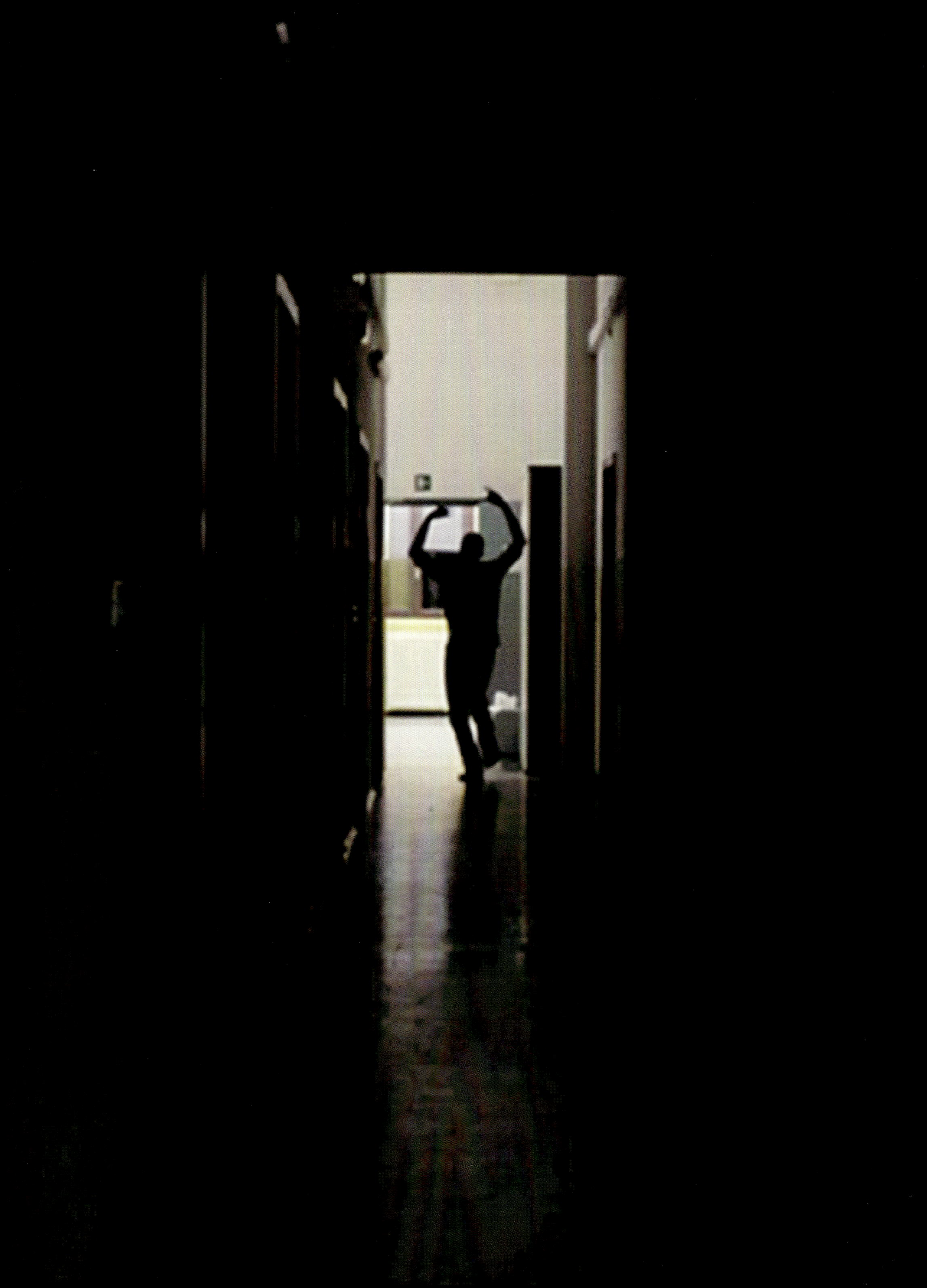

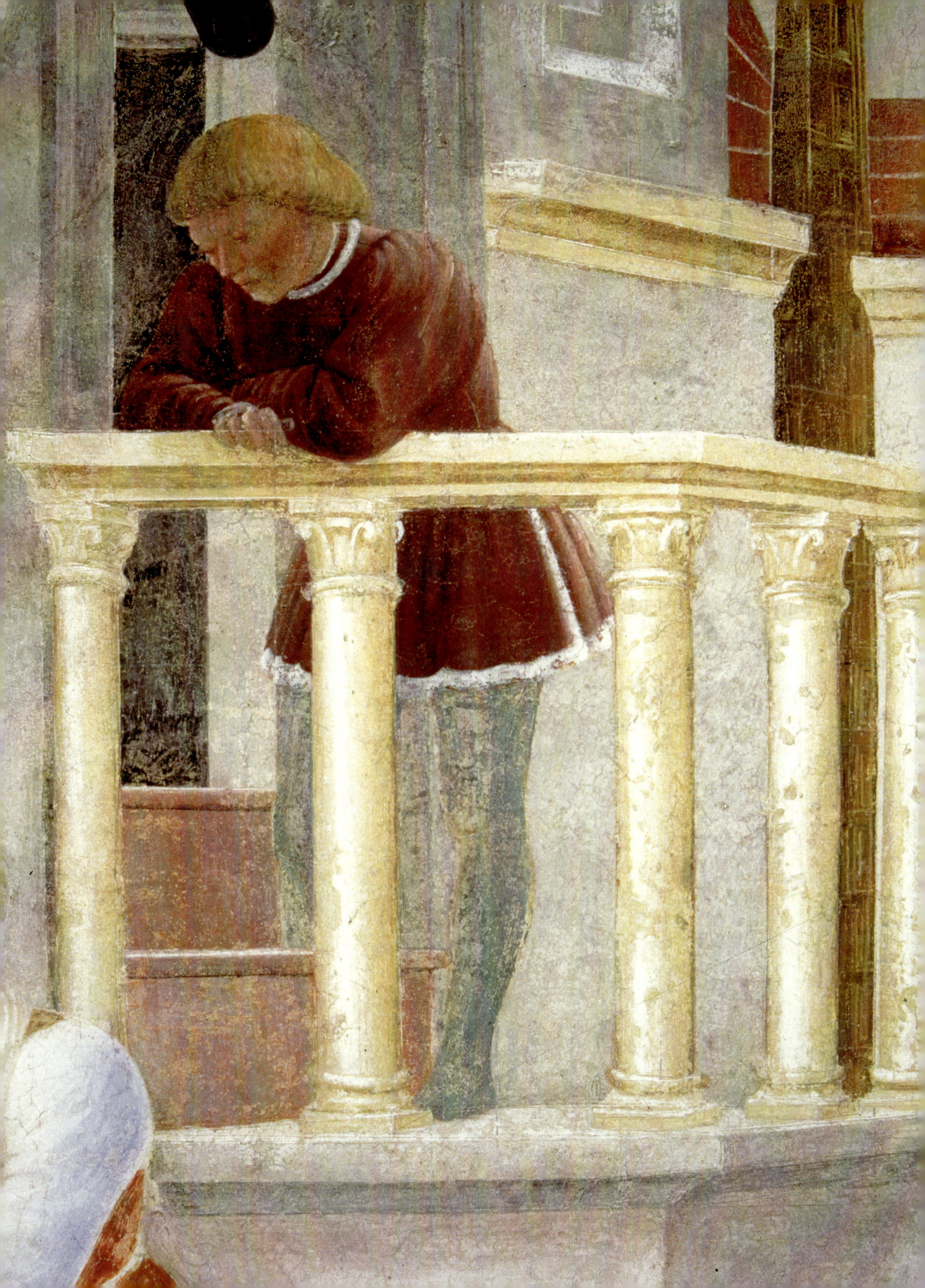

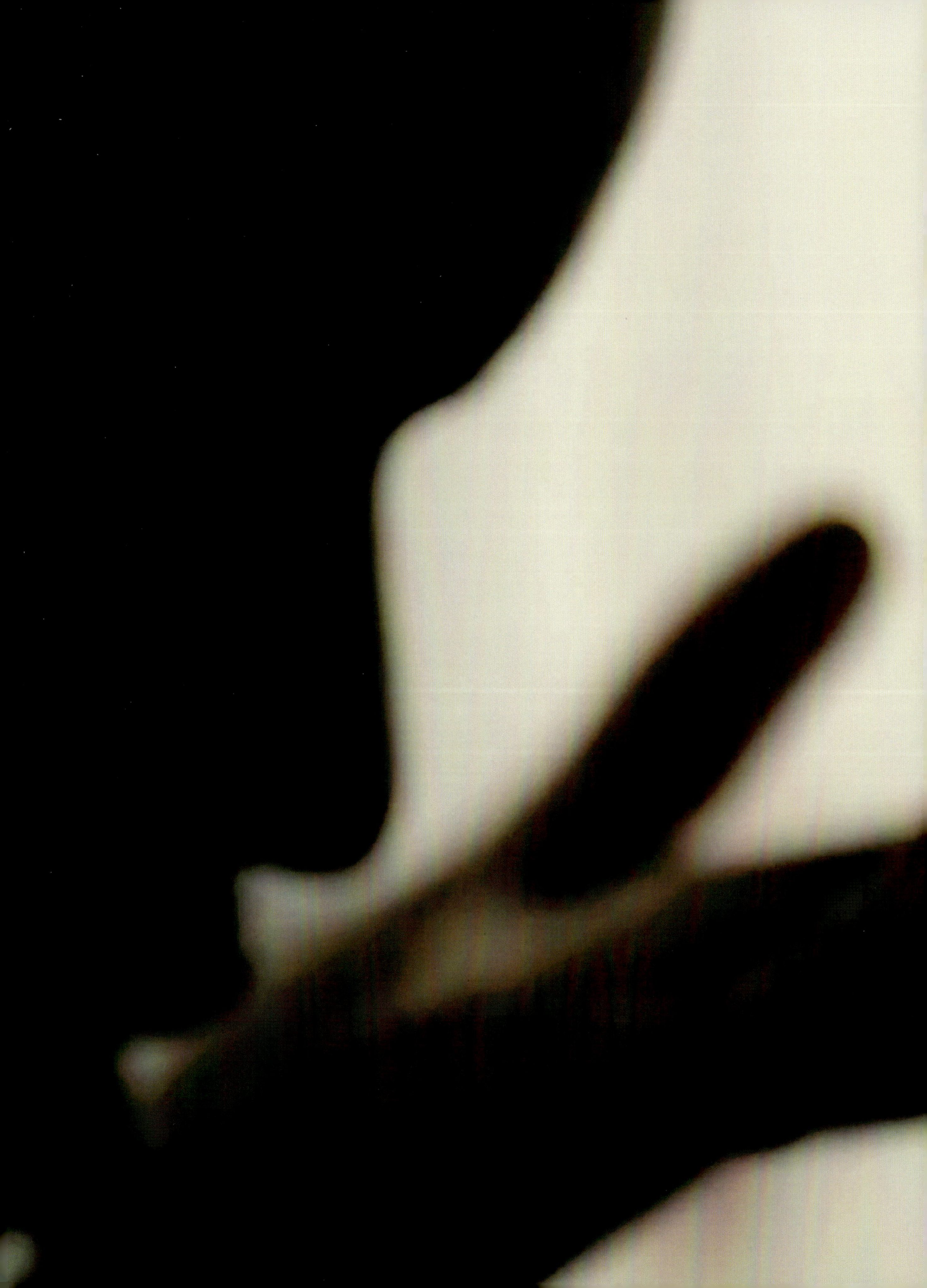

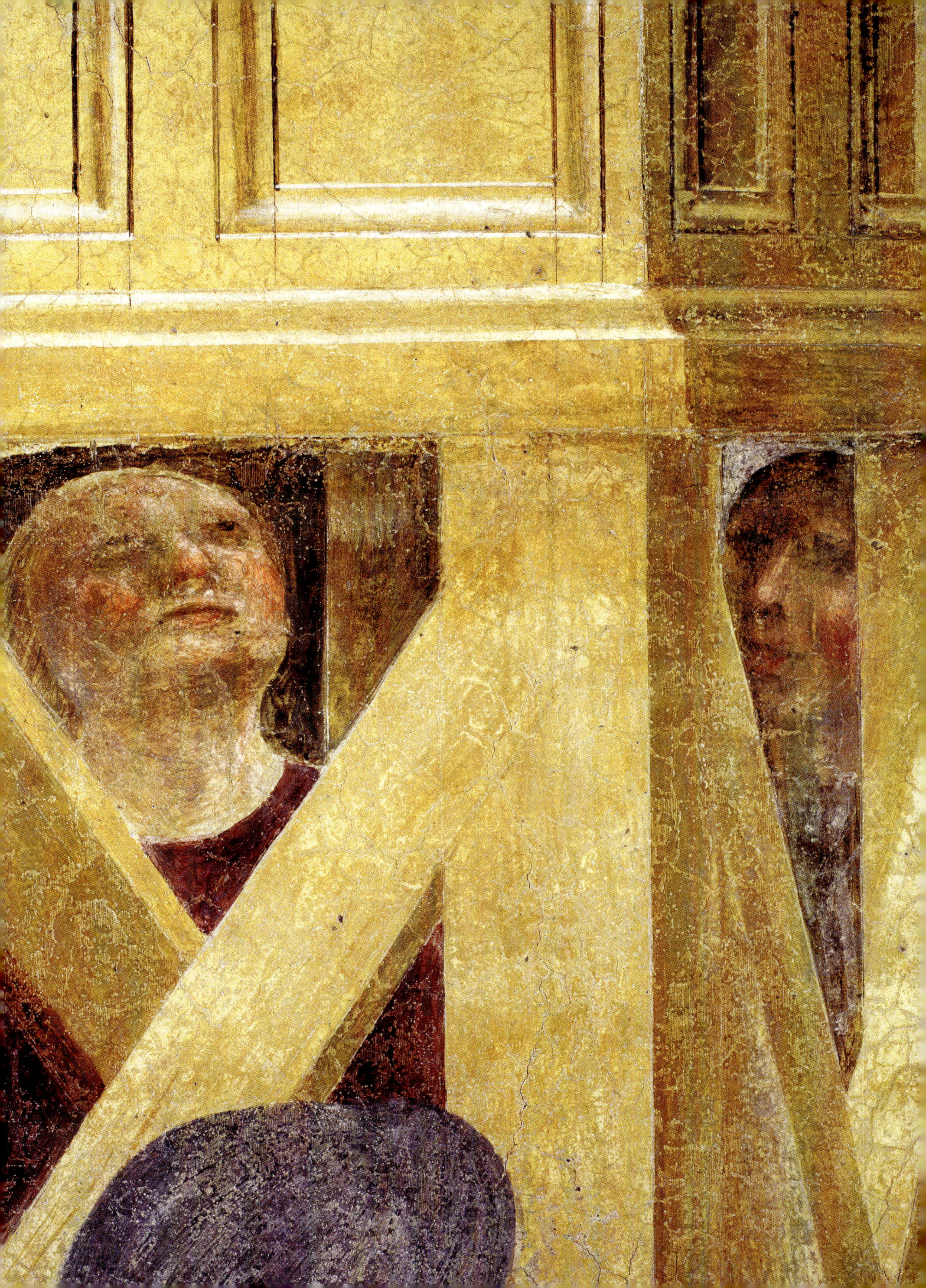

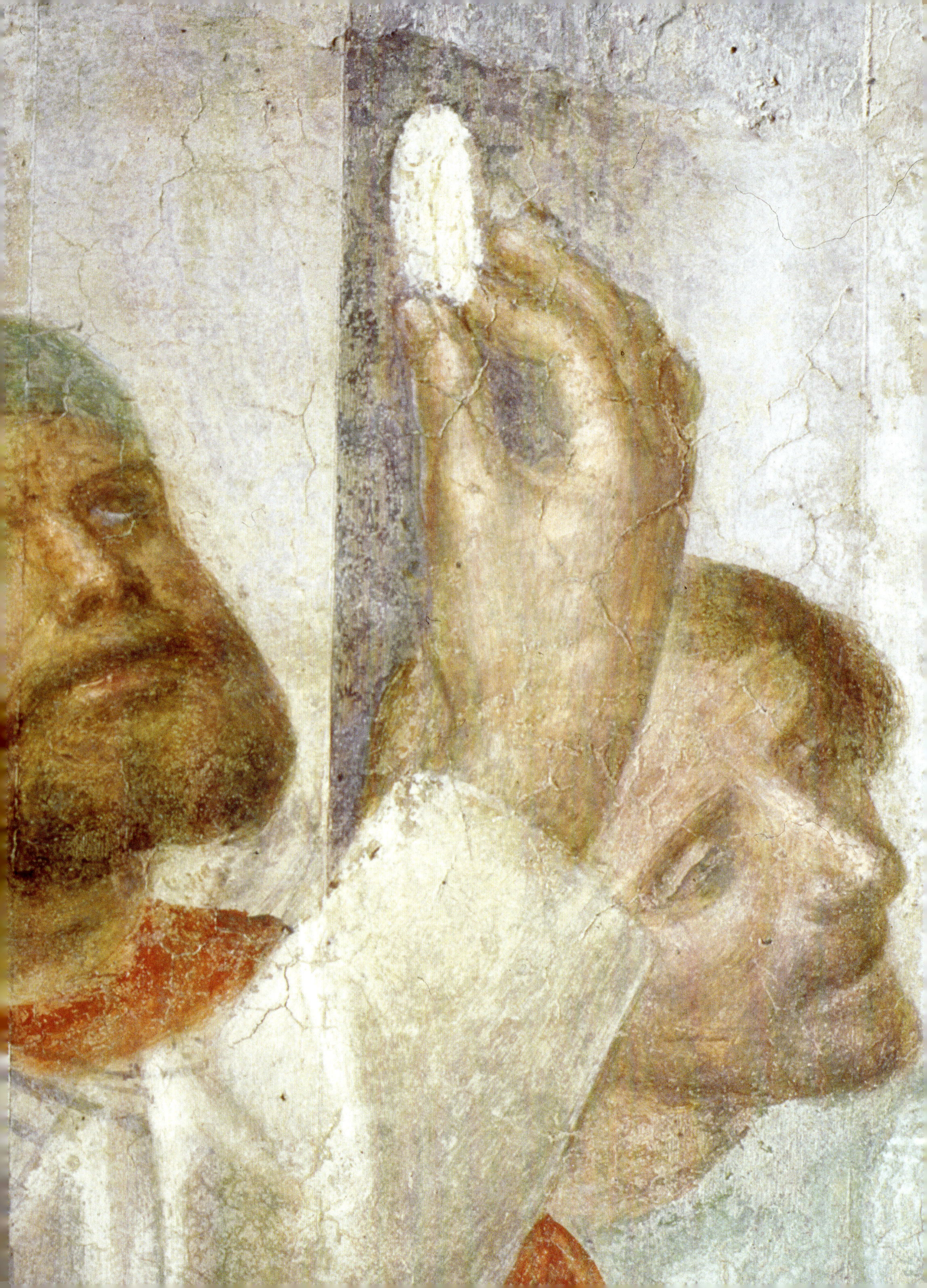

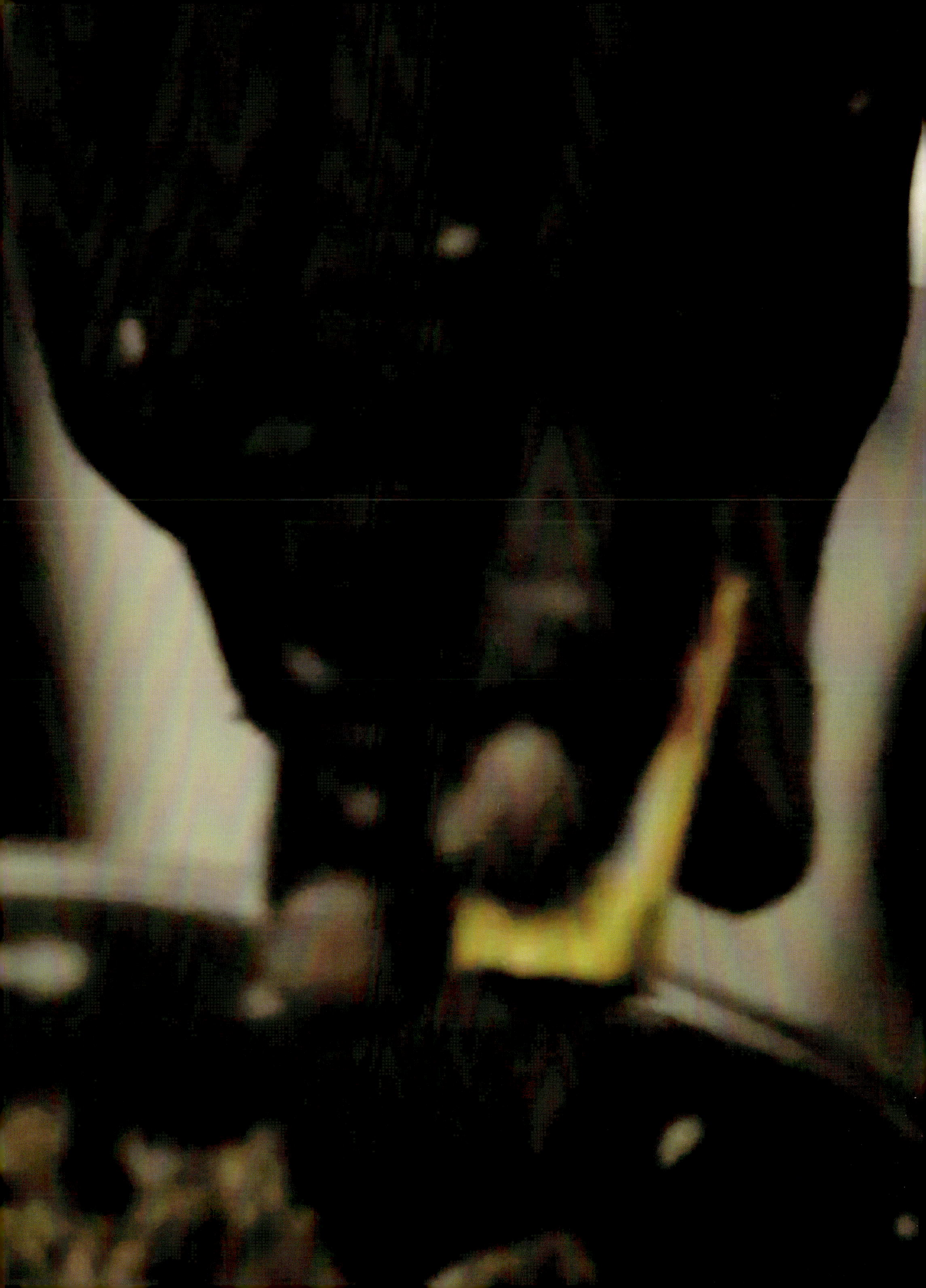

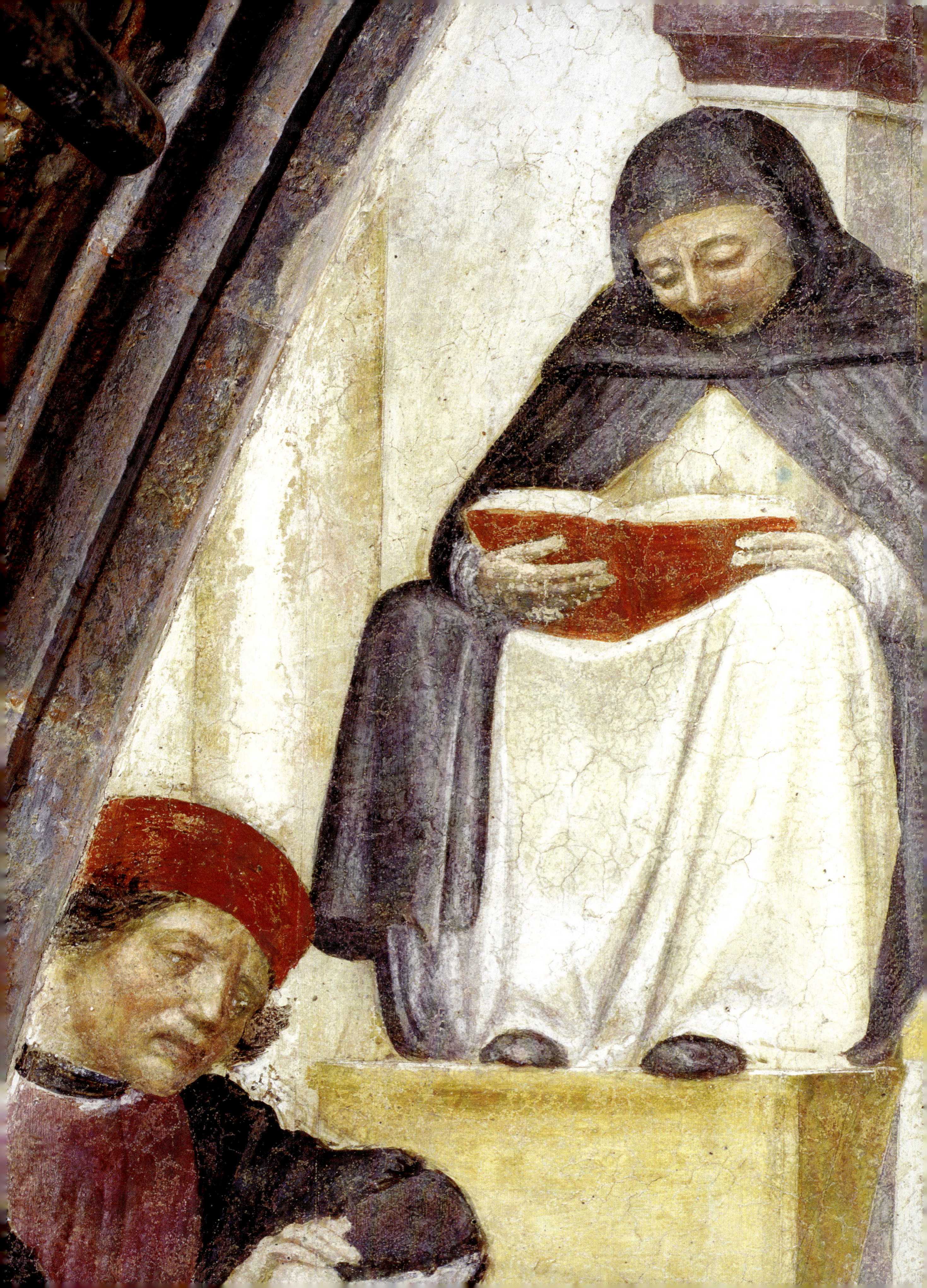

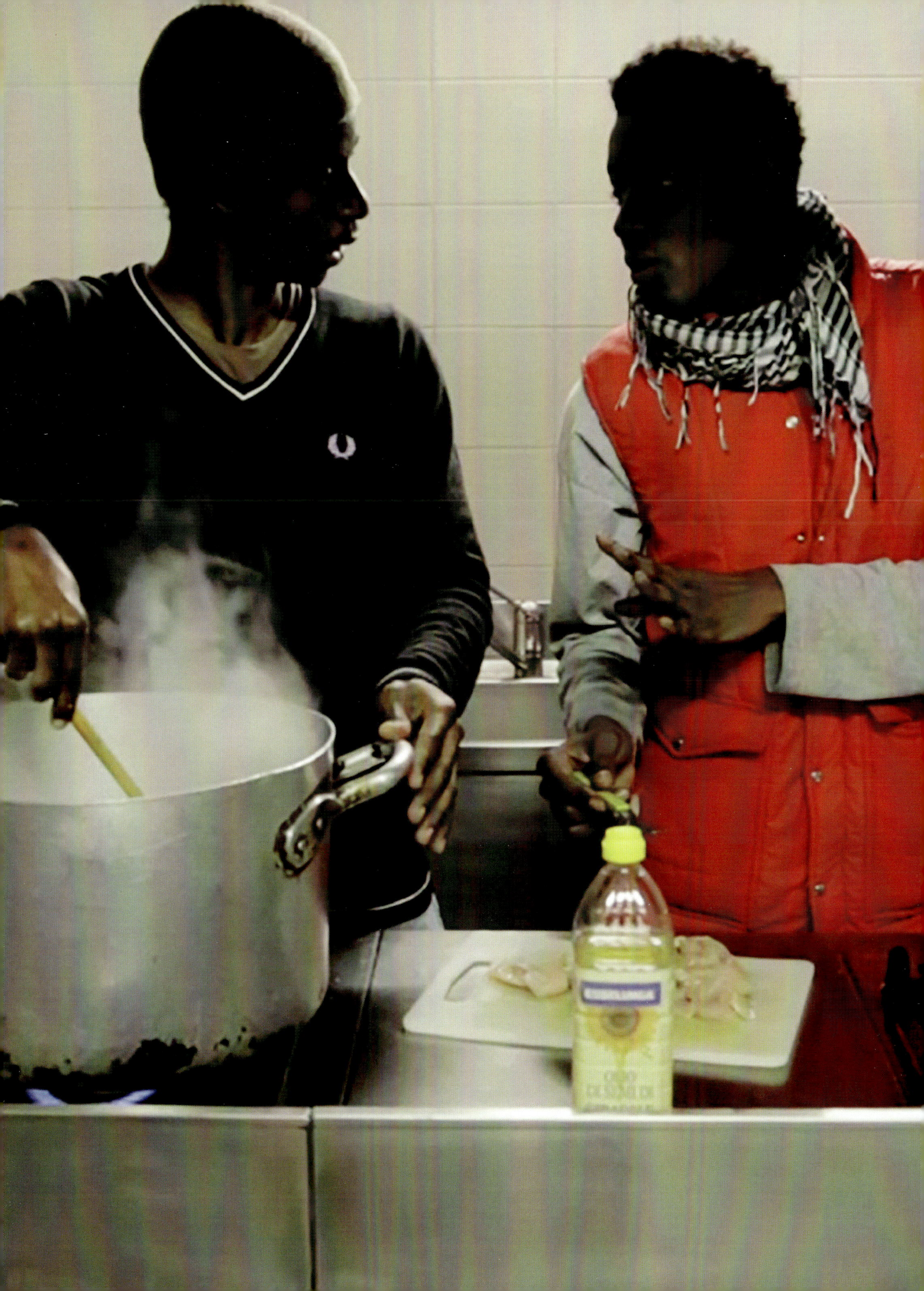

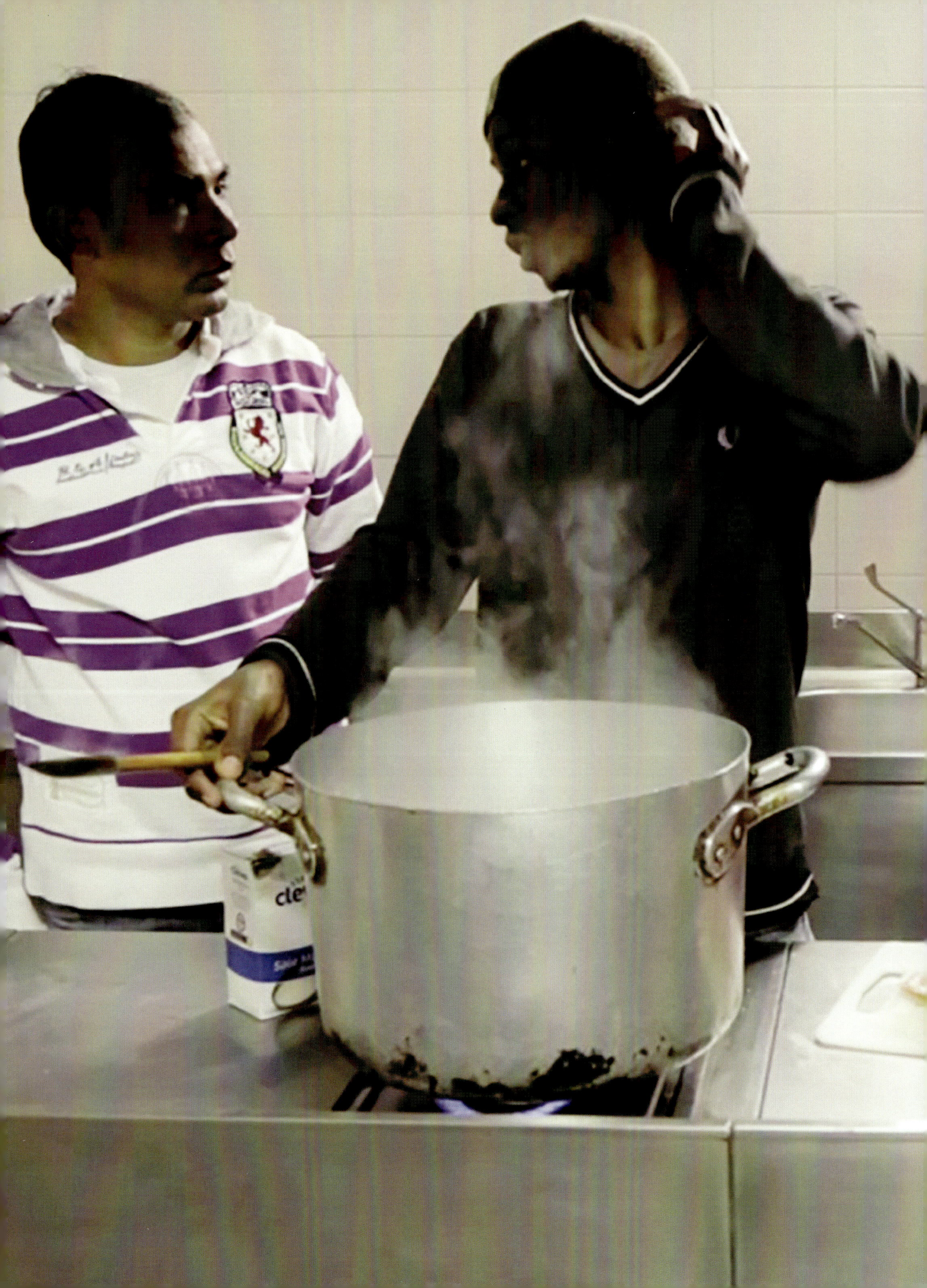

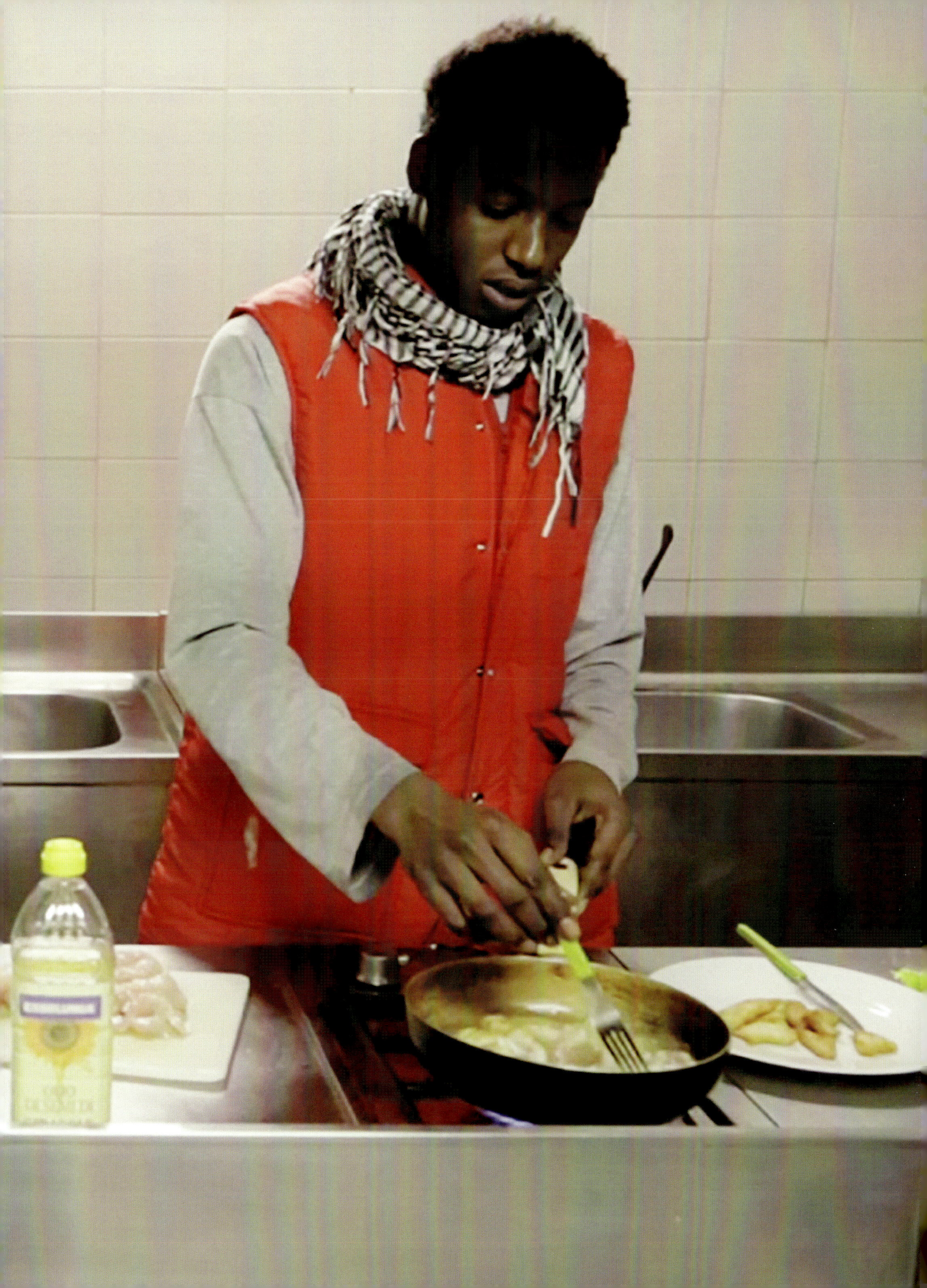

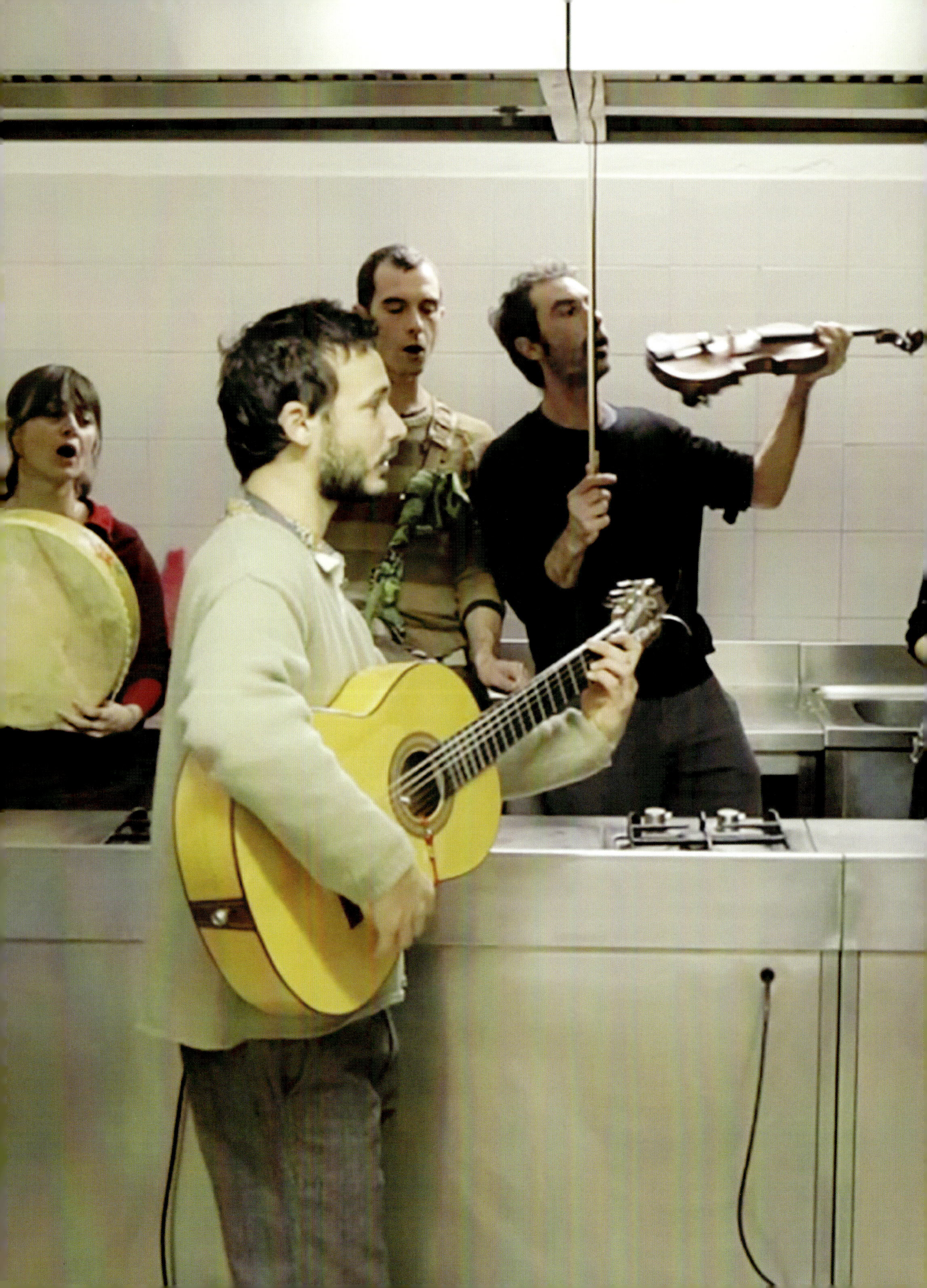

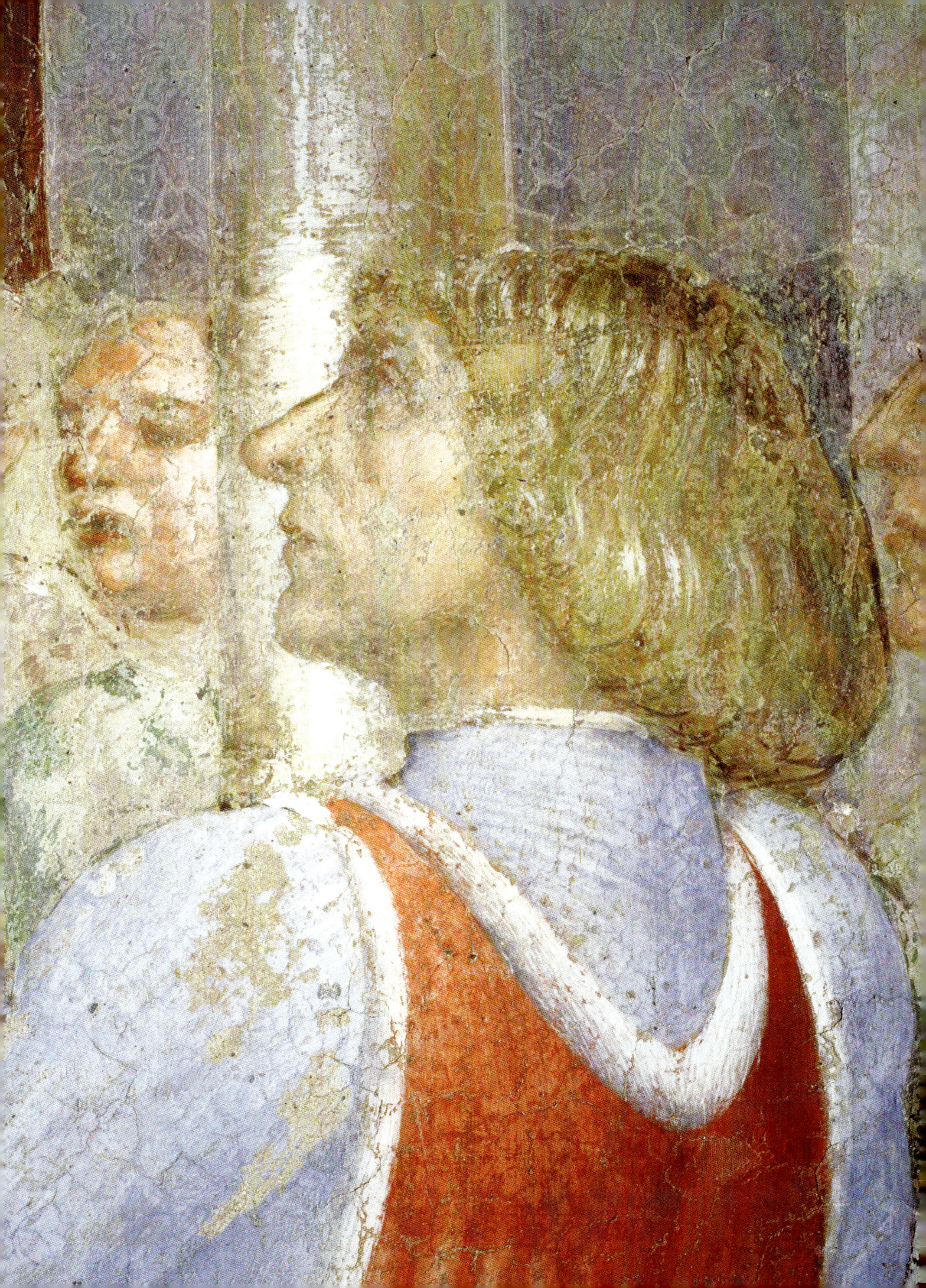

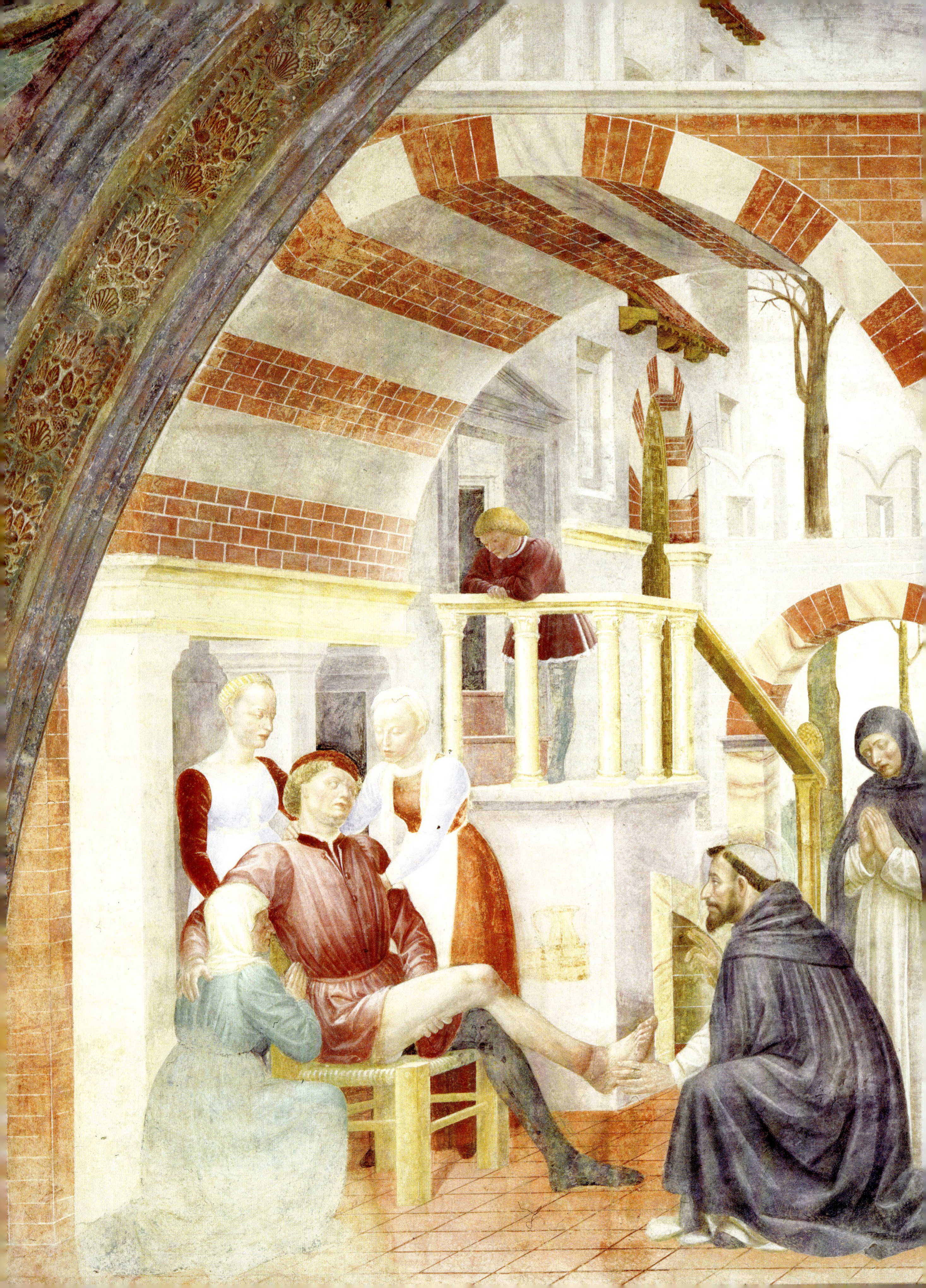

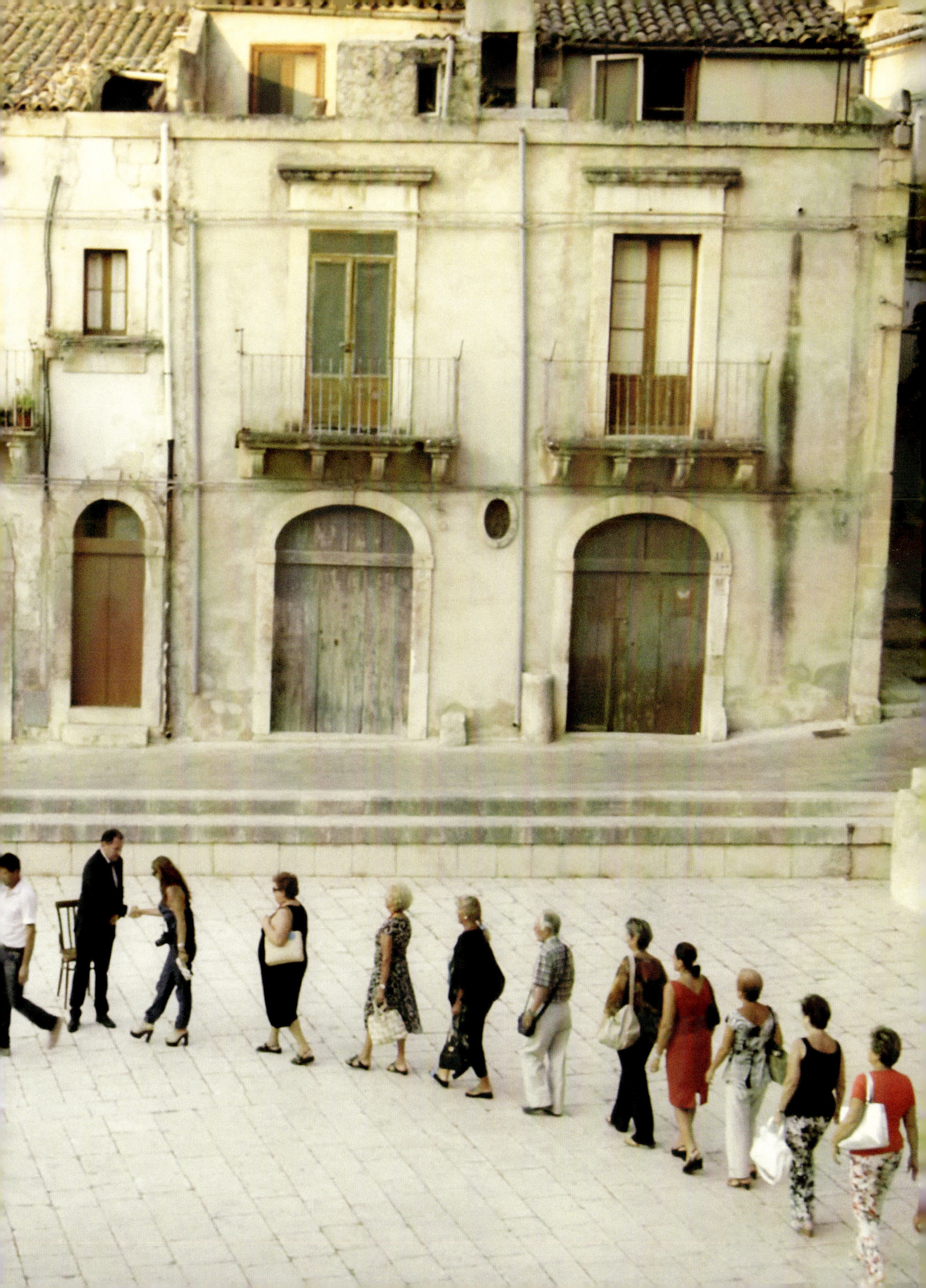

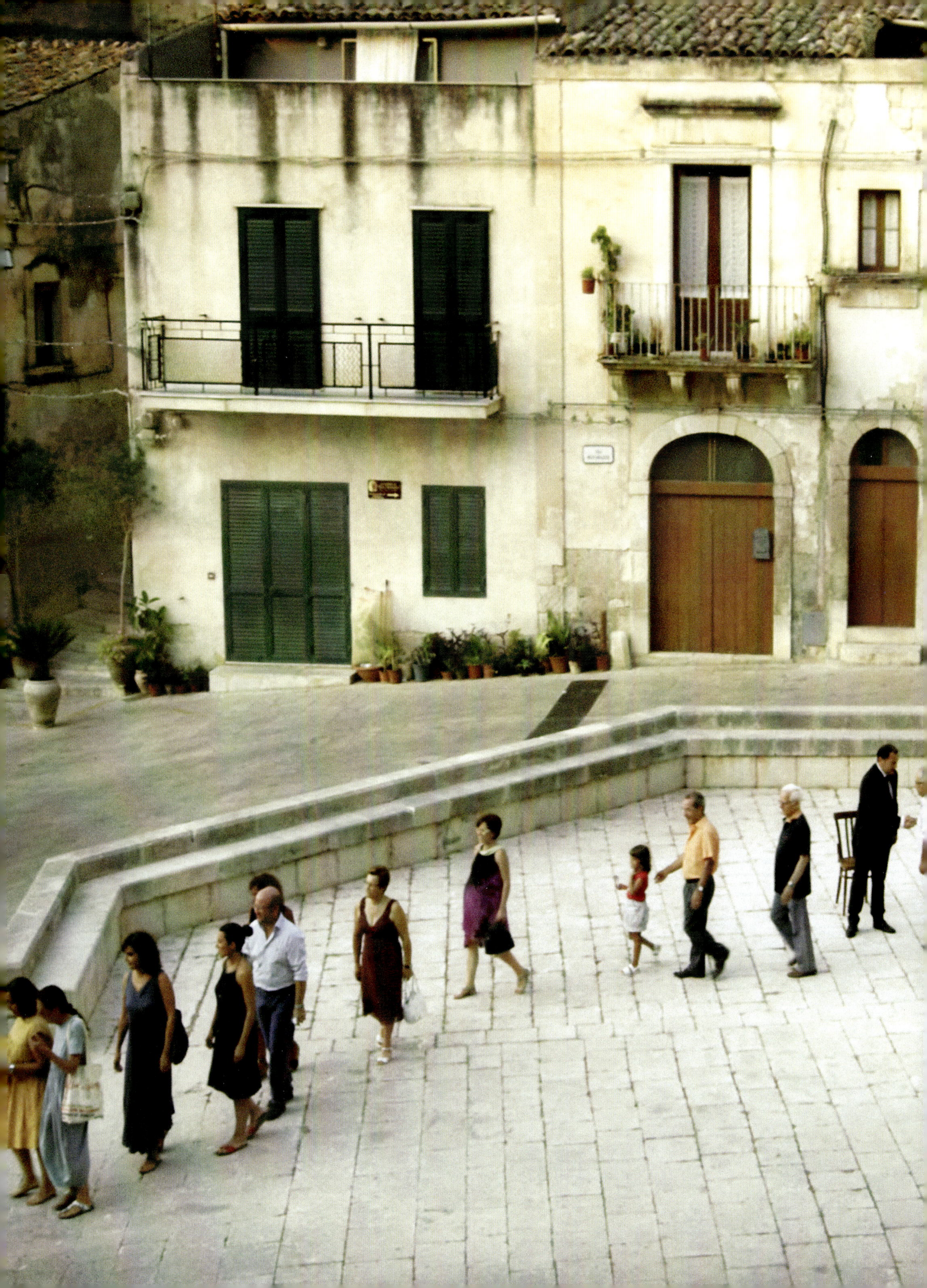

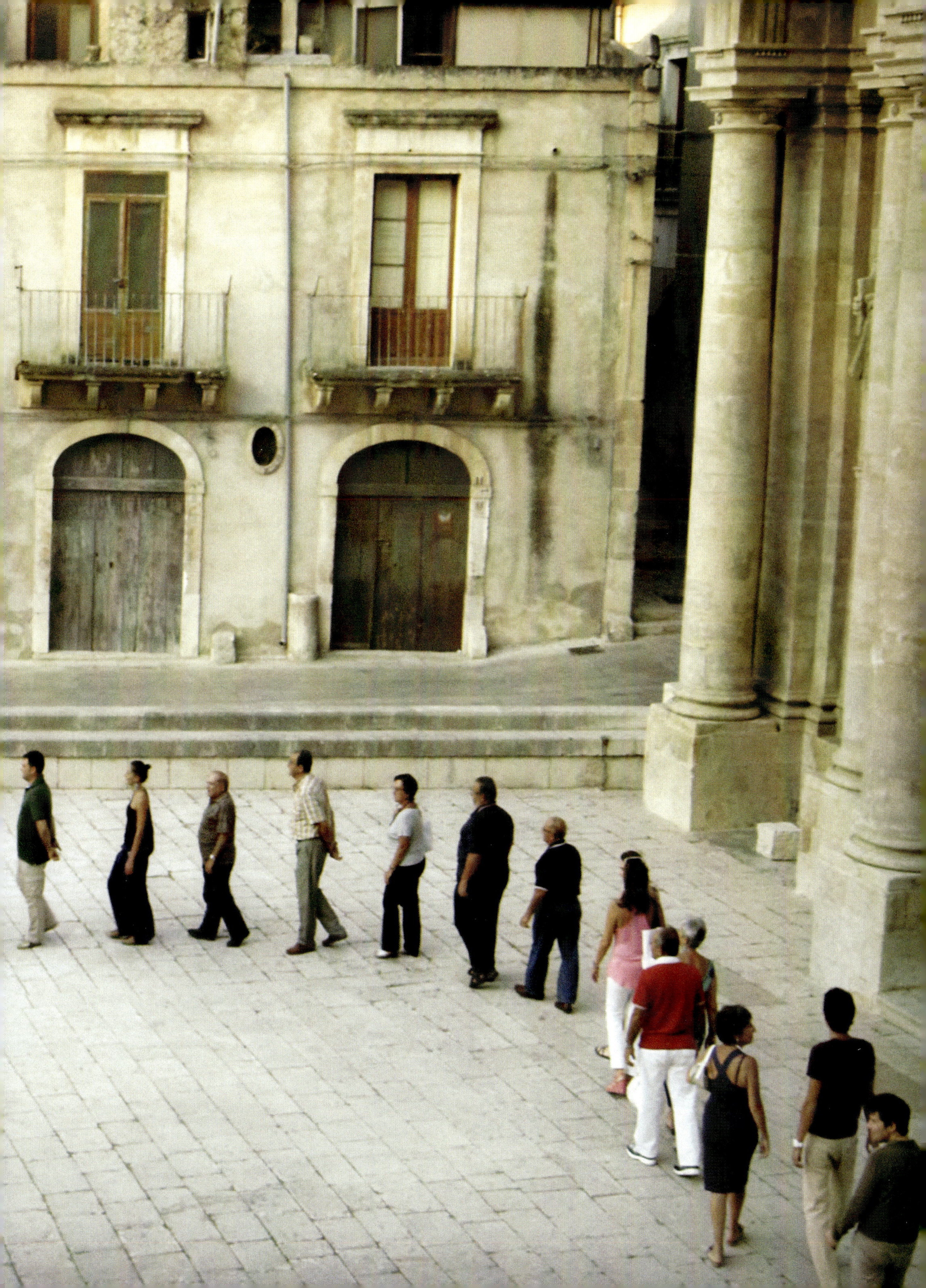

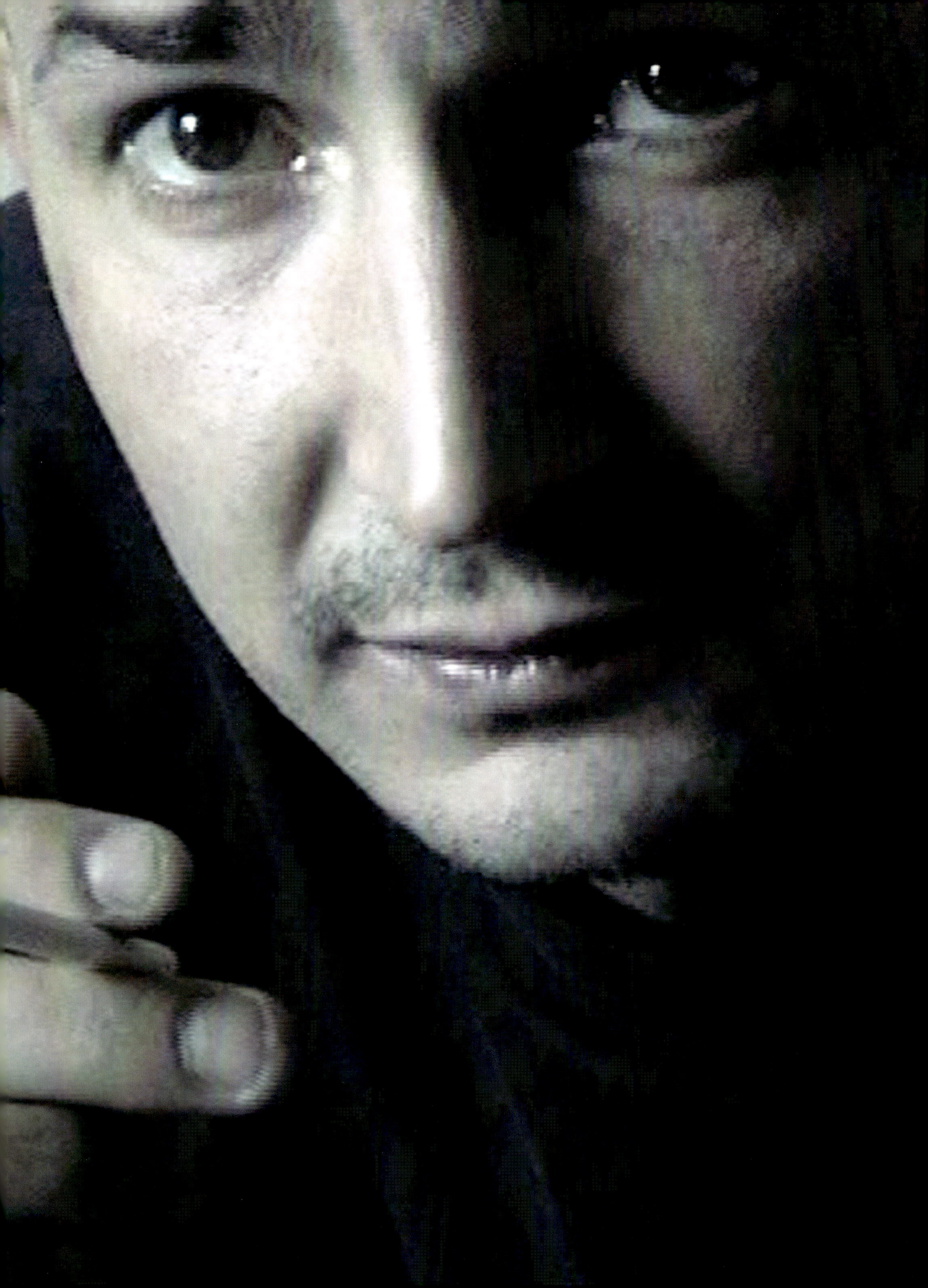

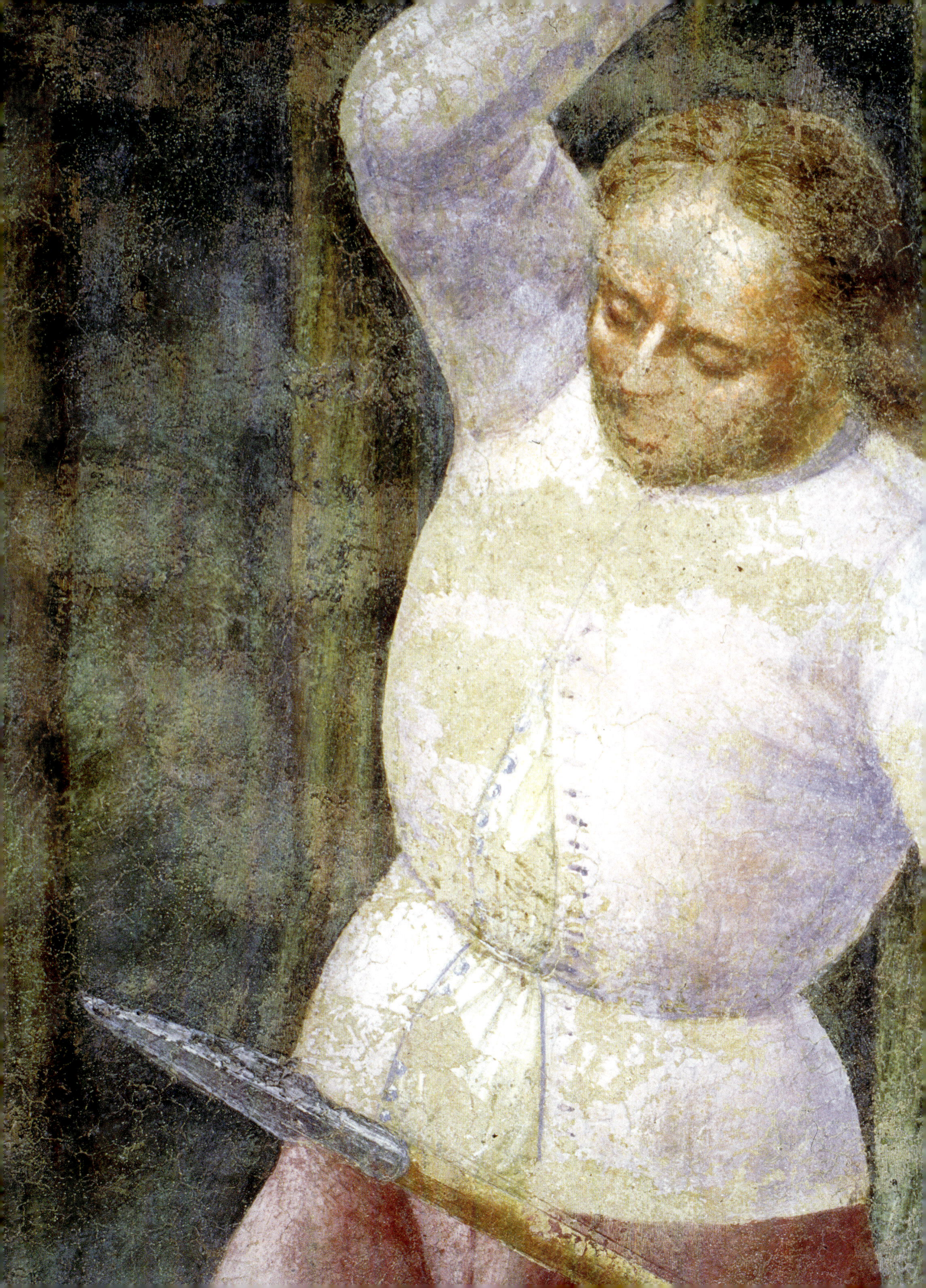

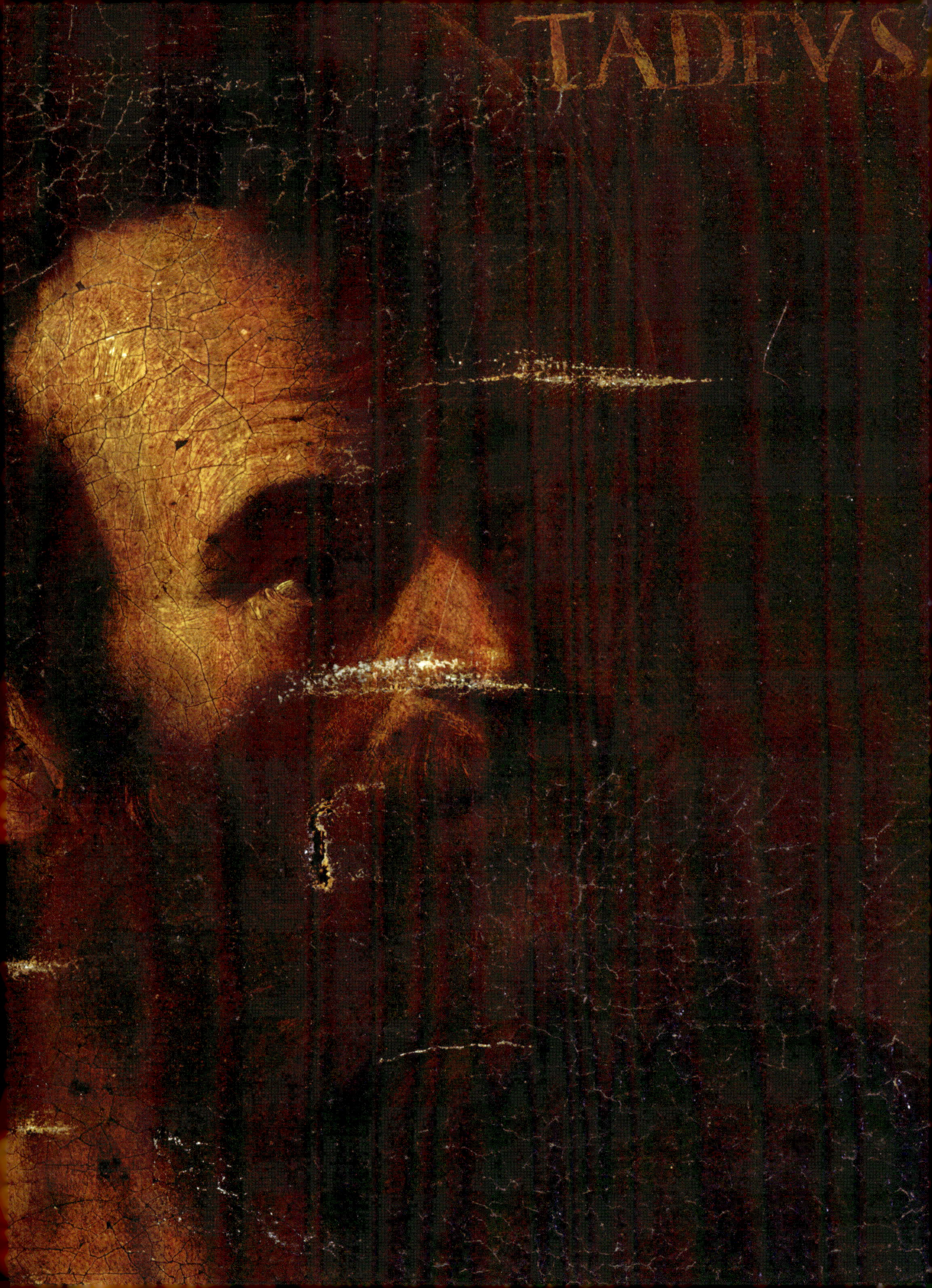
TADEVS

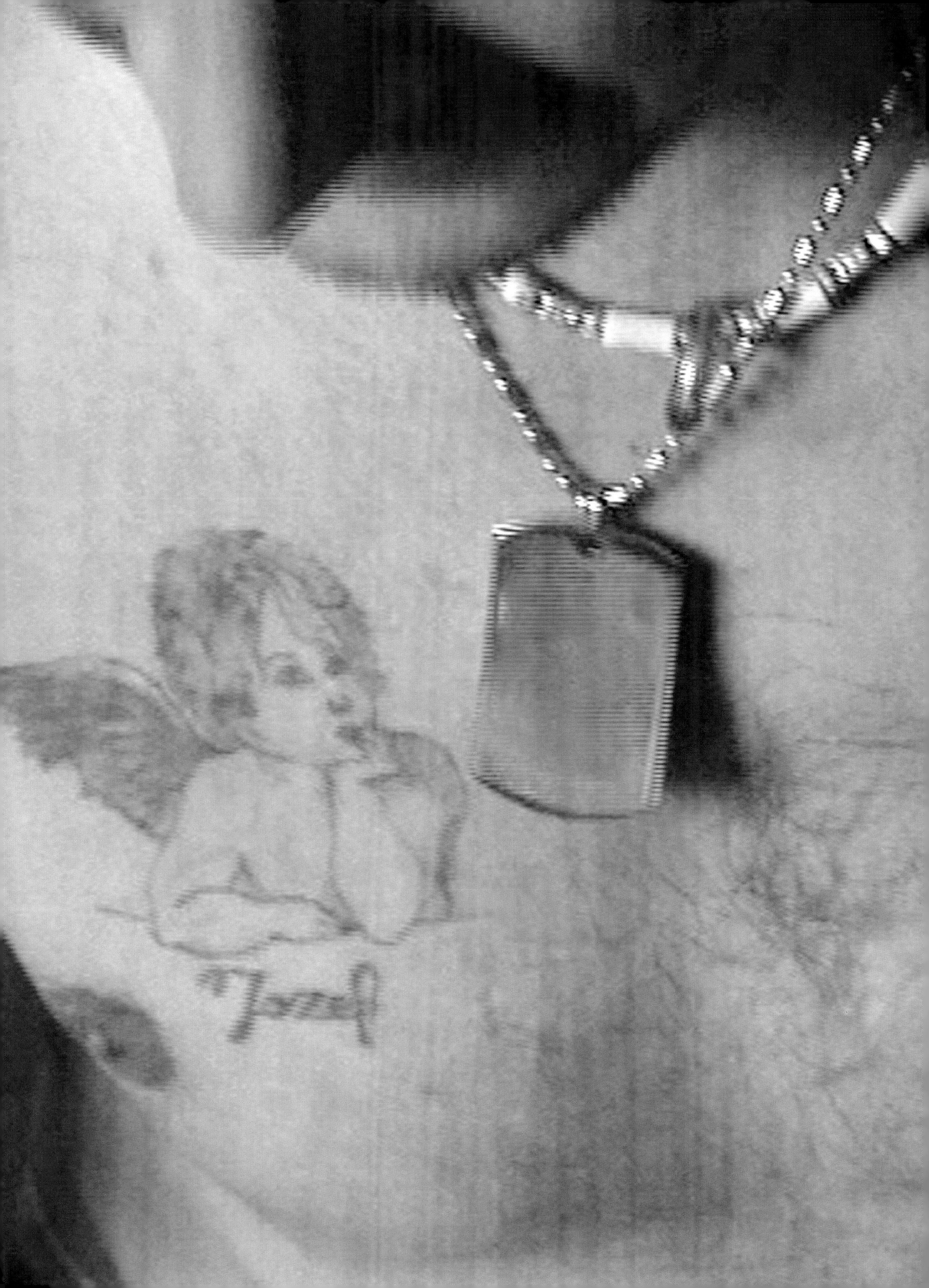

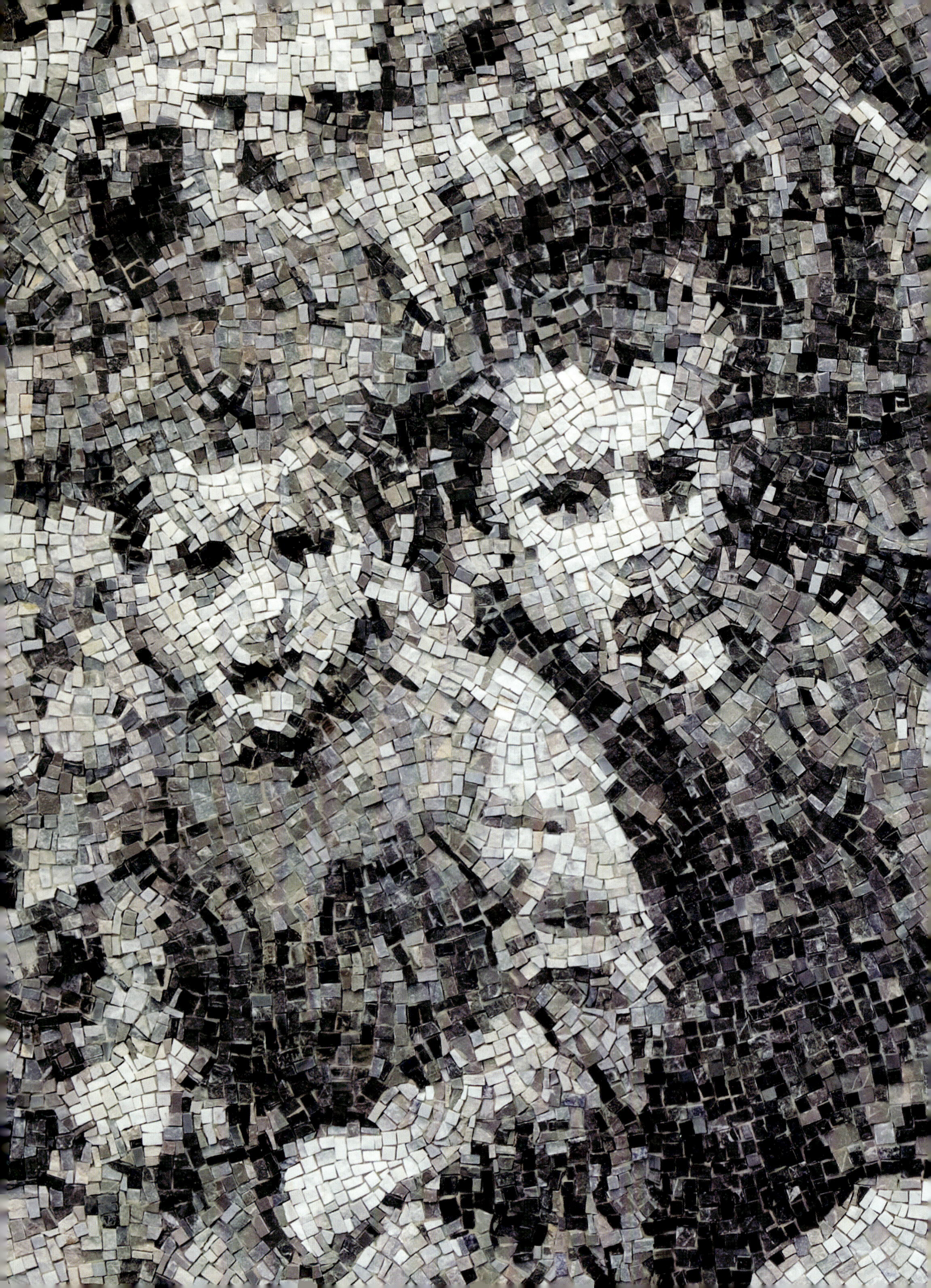

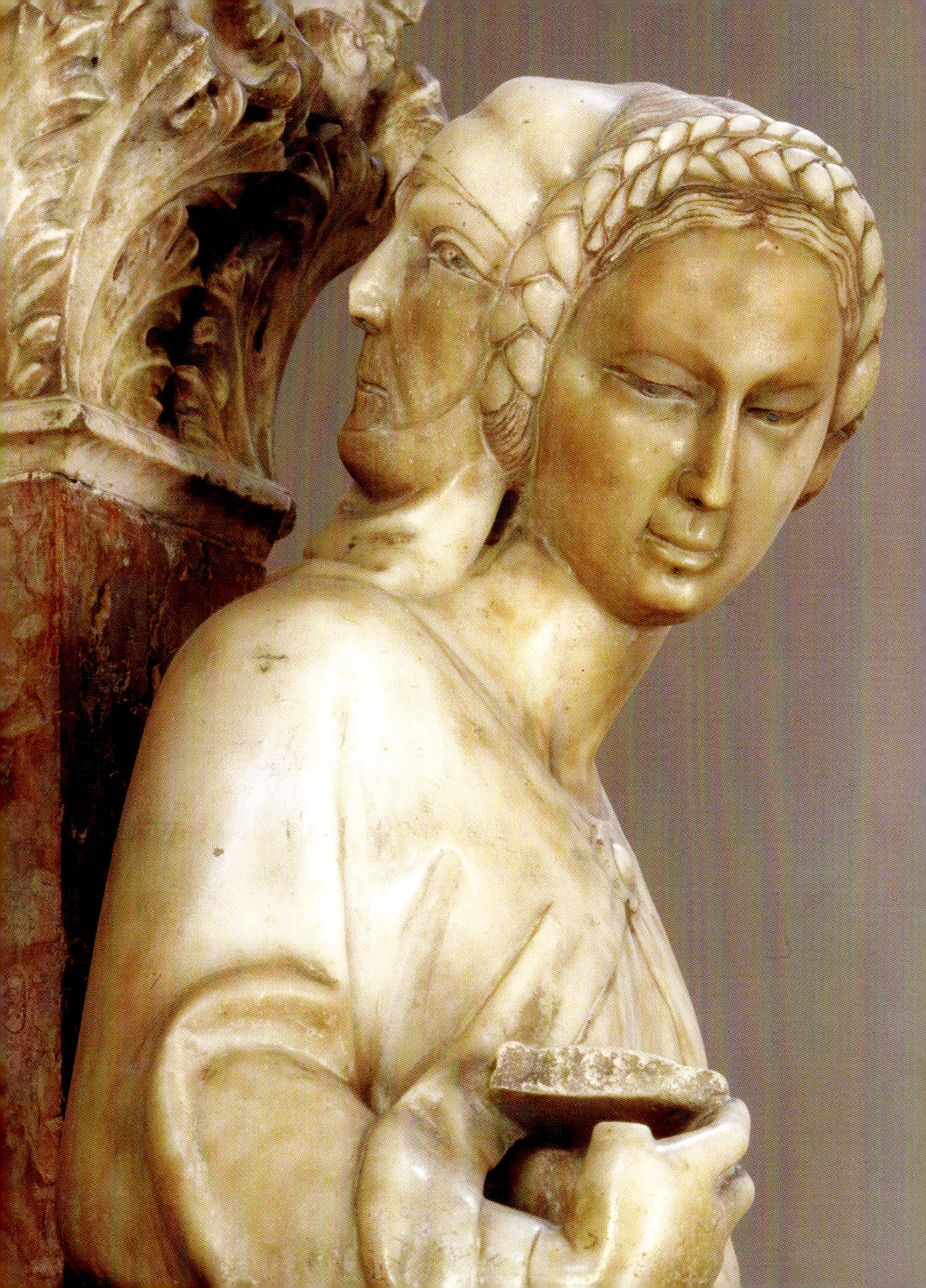

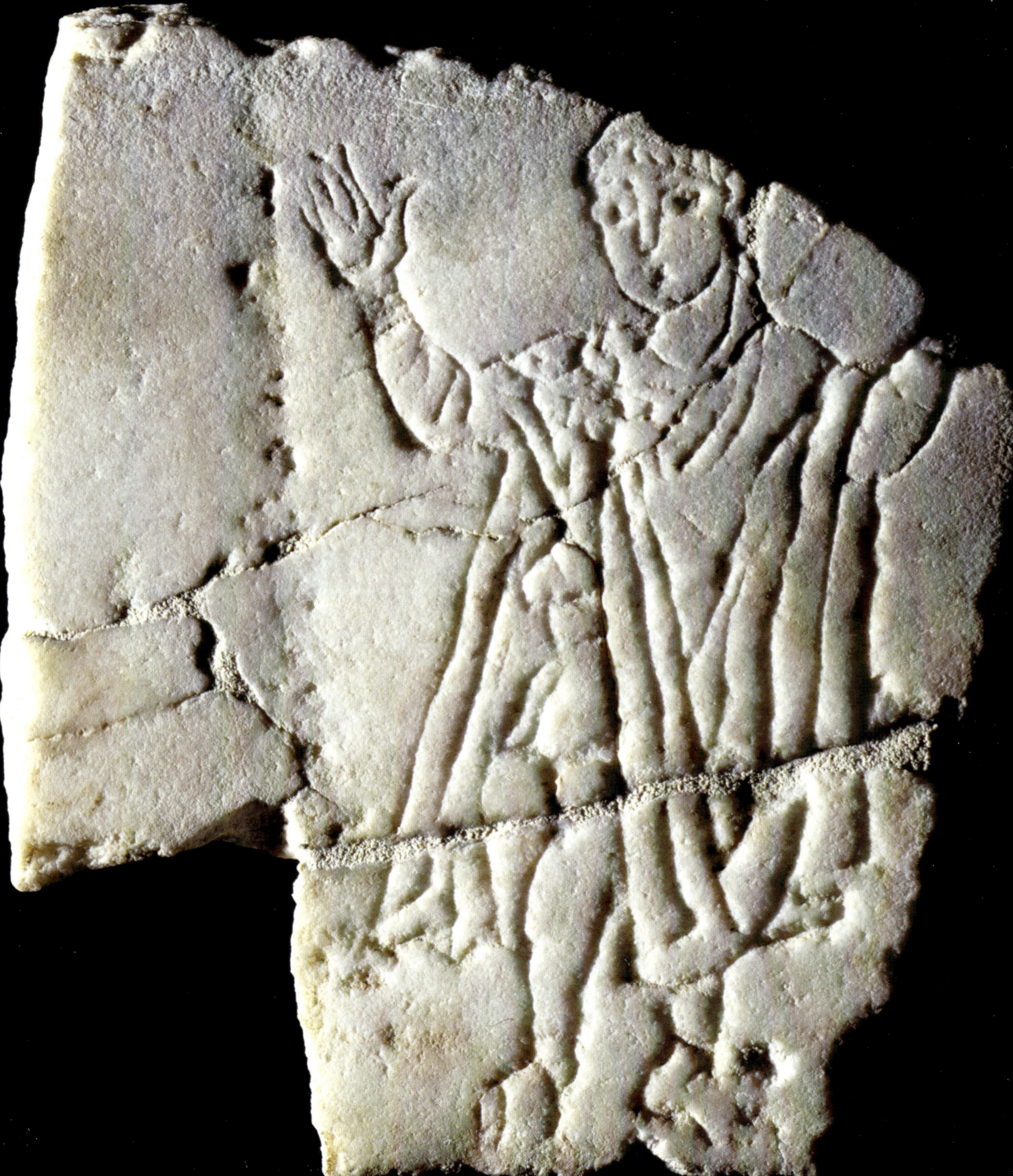

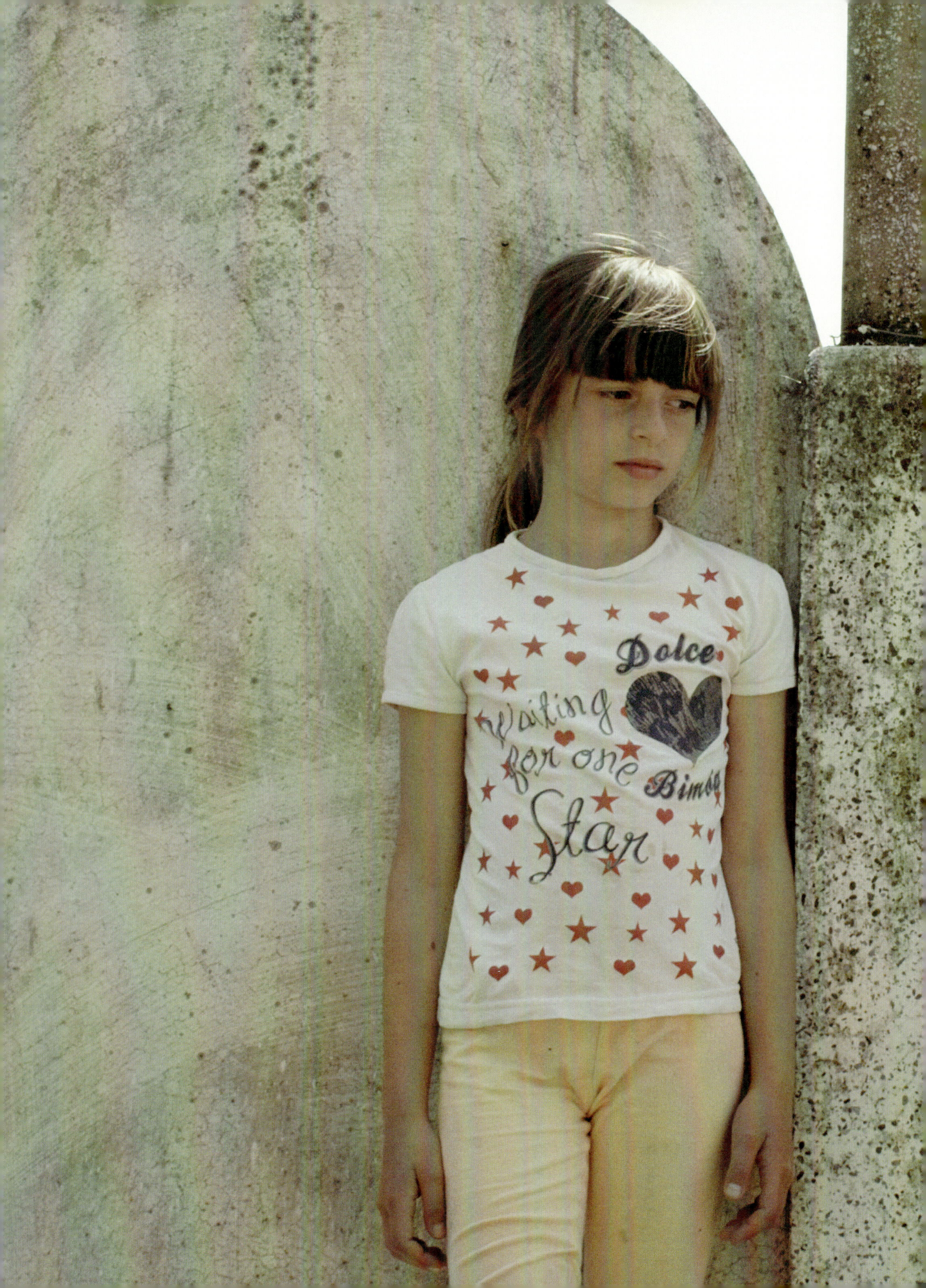
Dolce
waiting
for one
Star

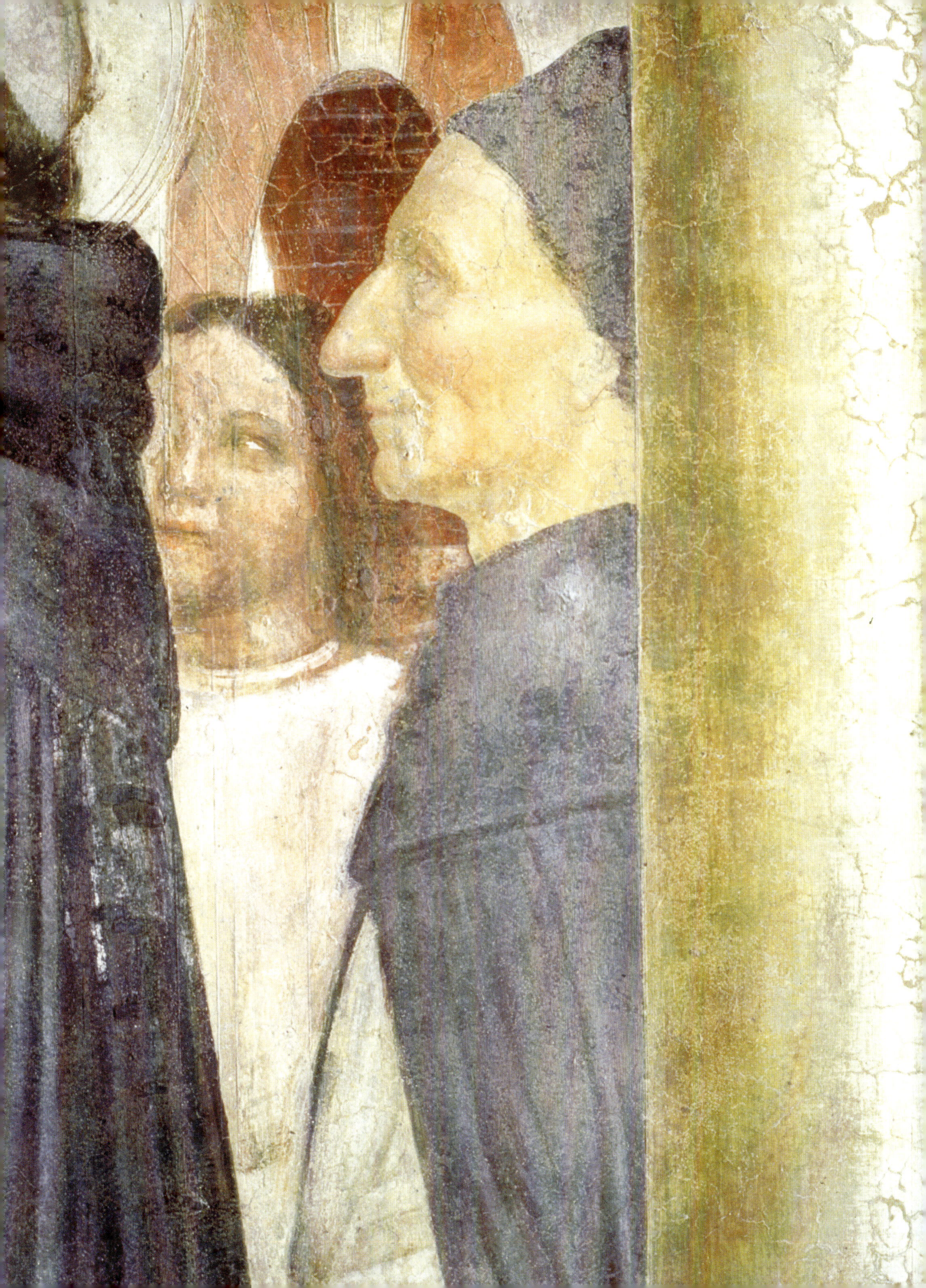

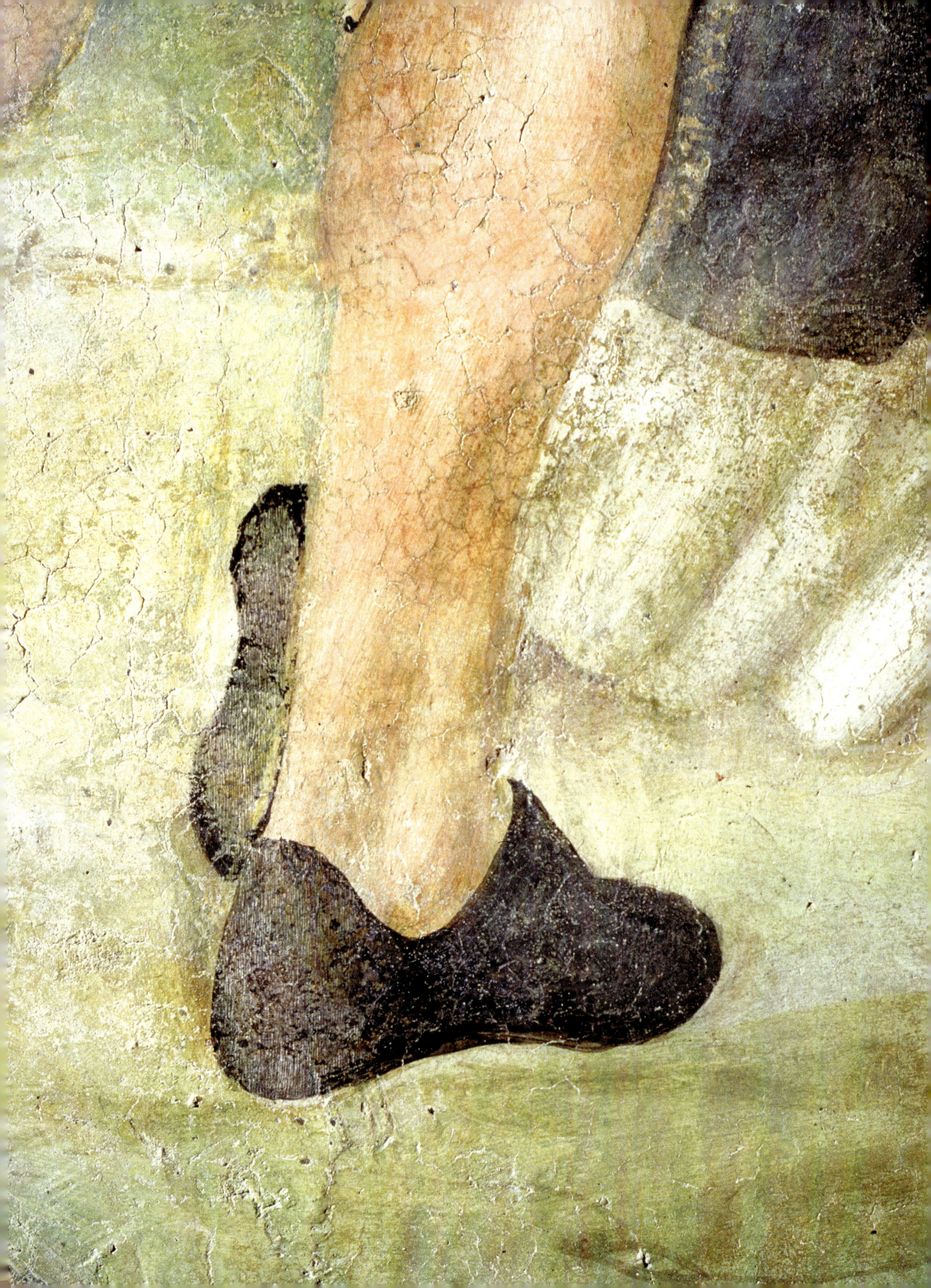

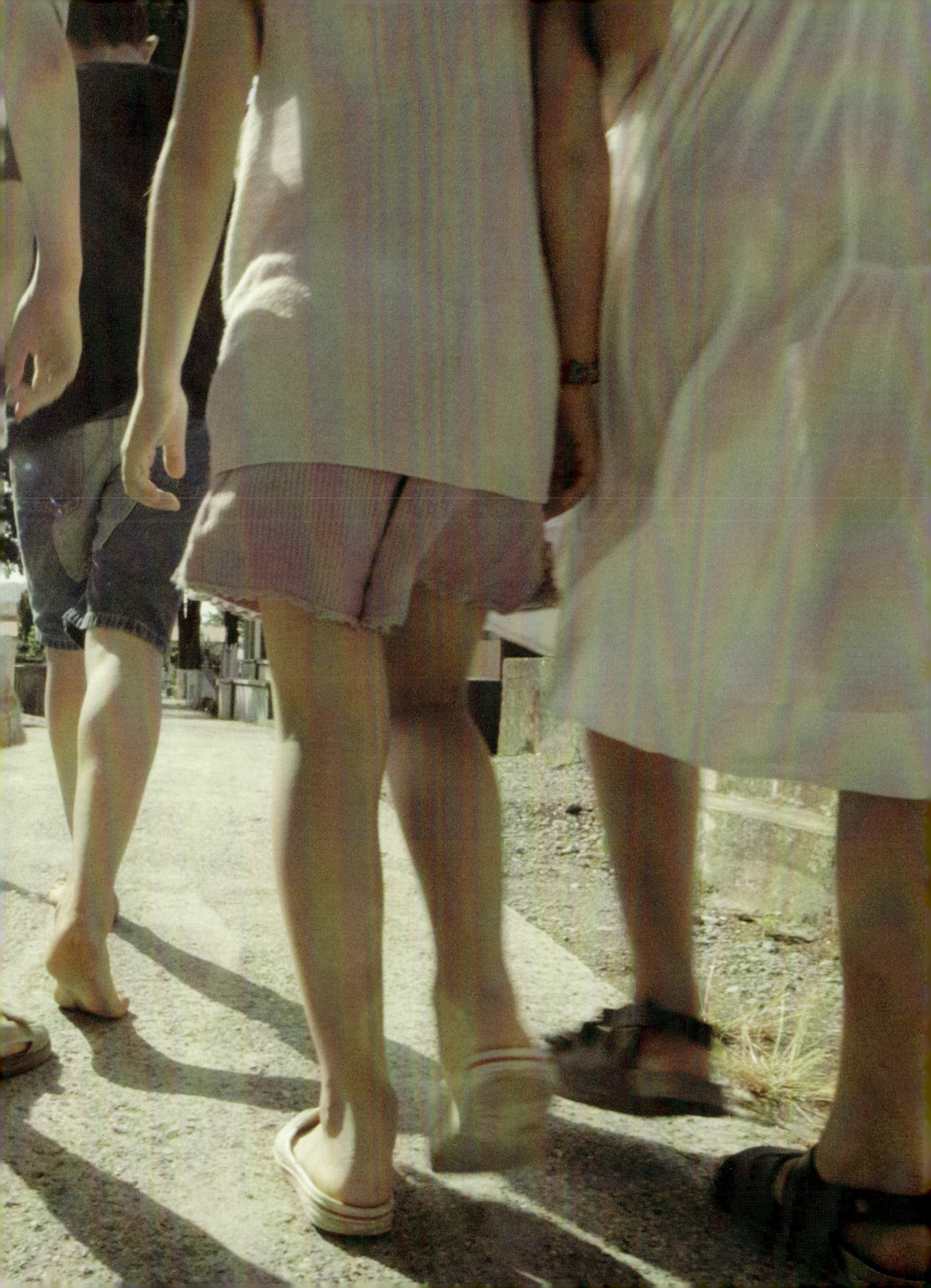

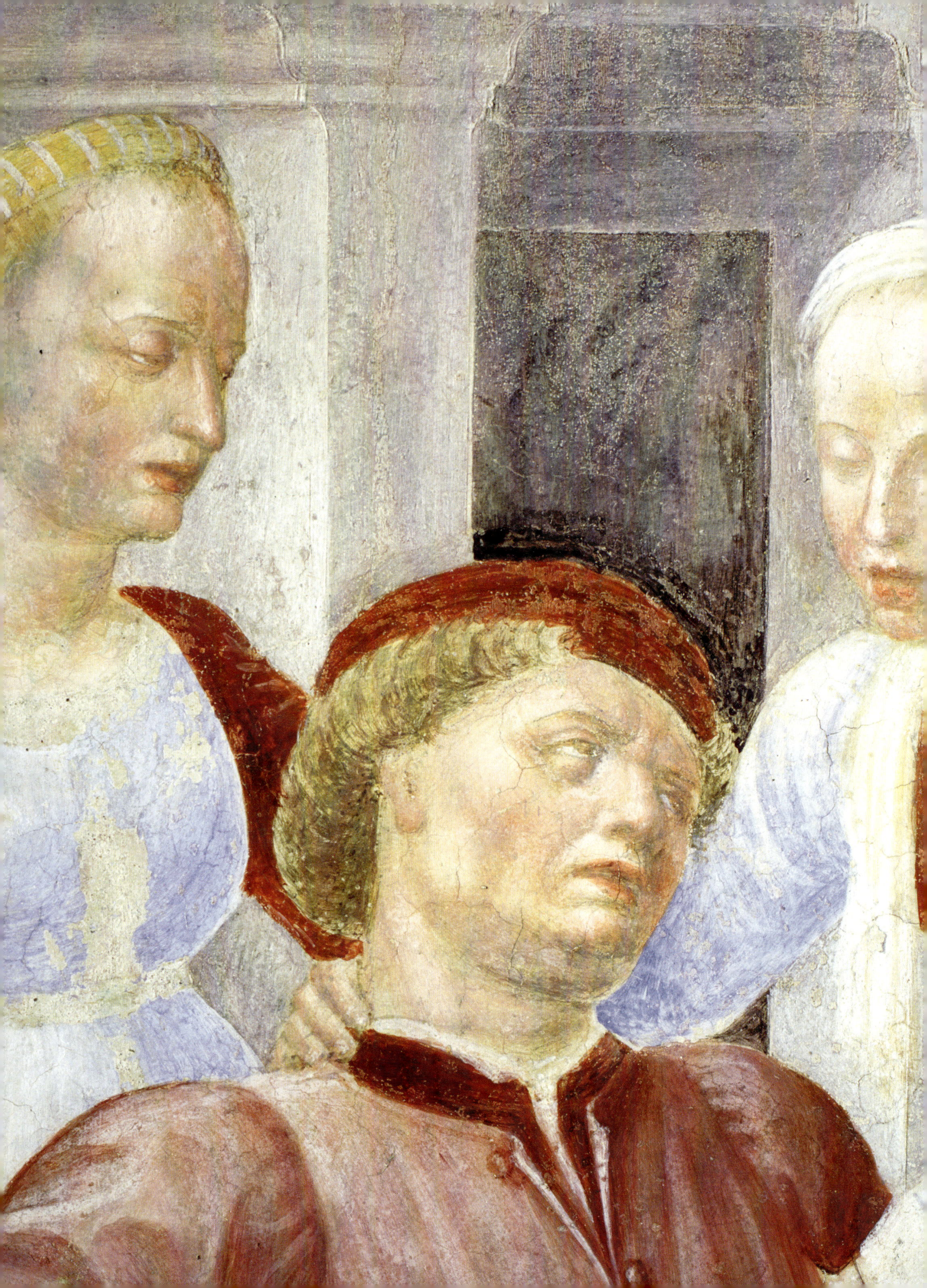

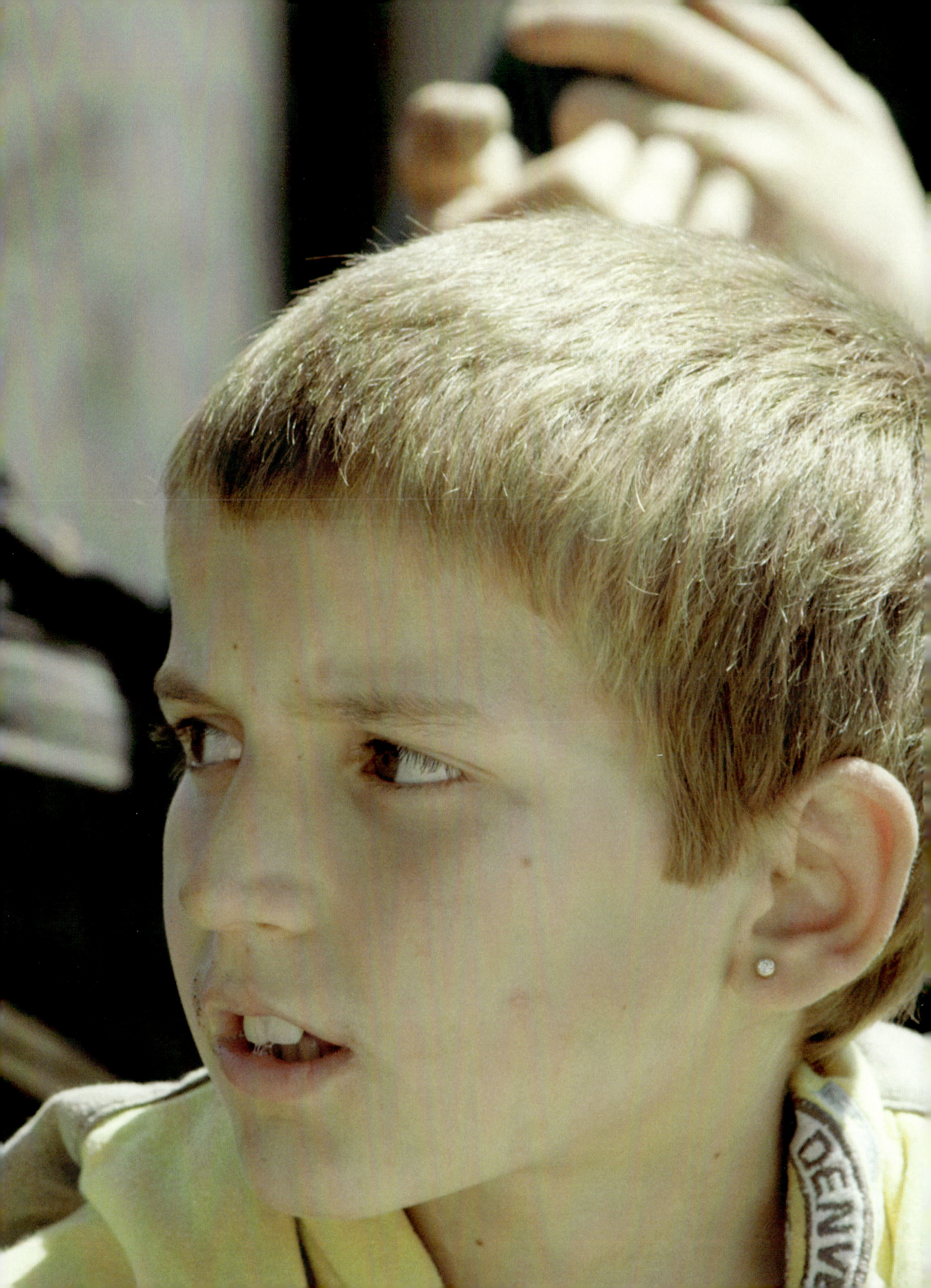

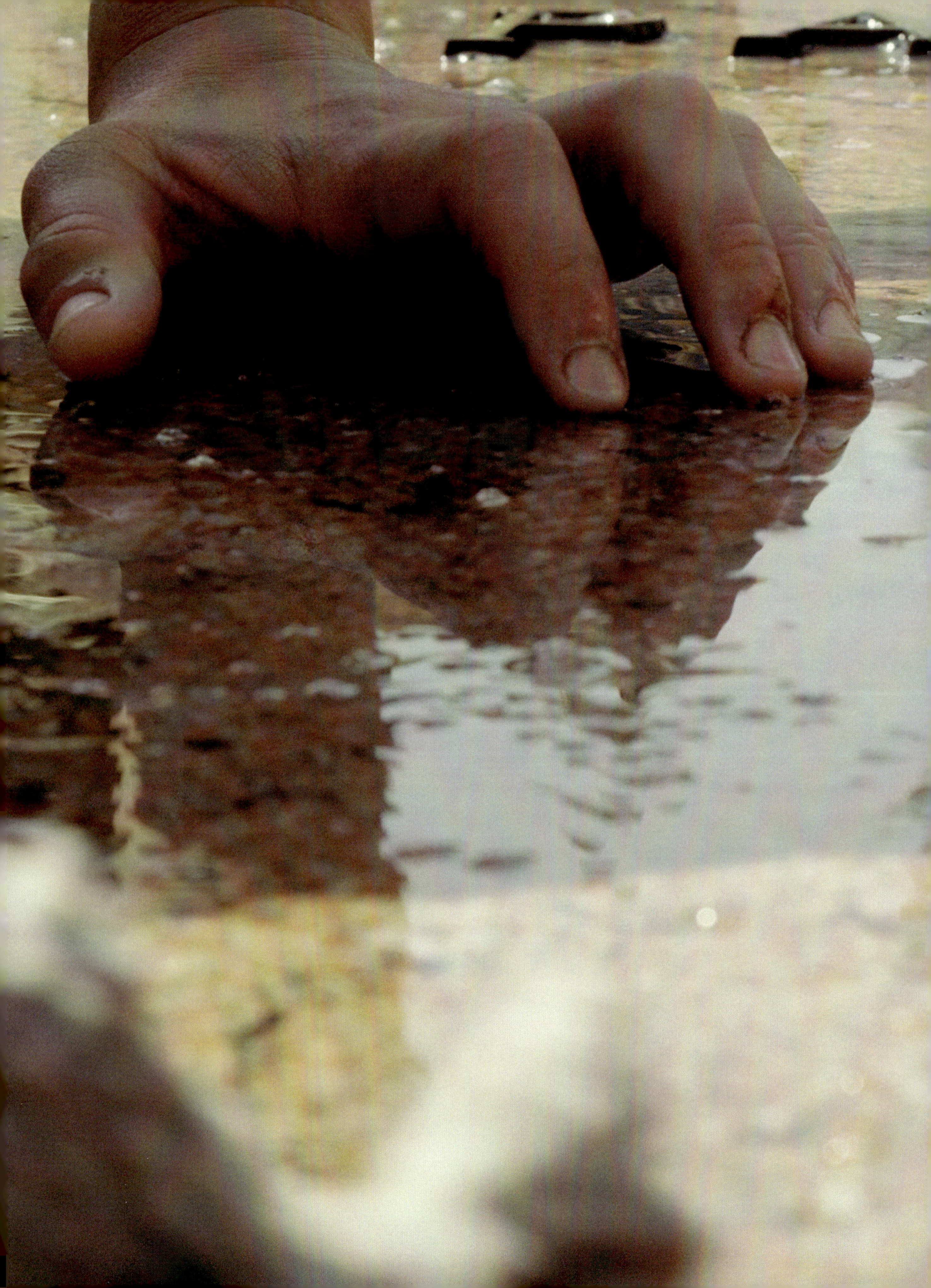

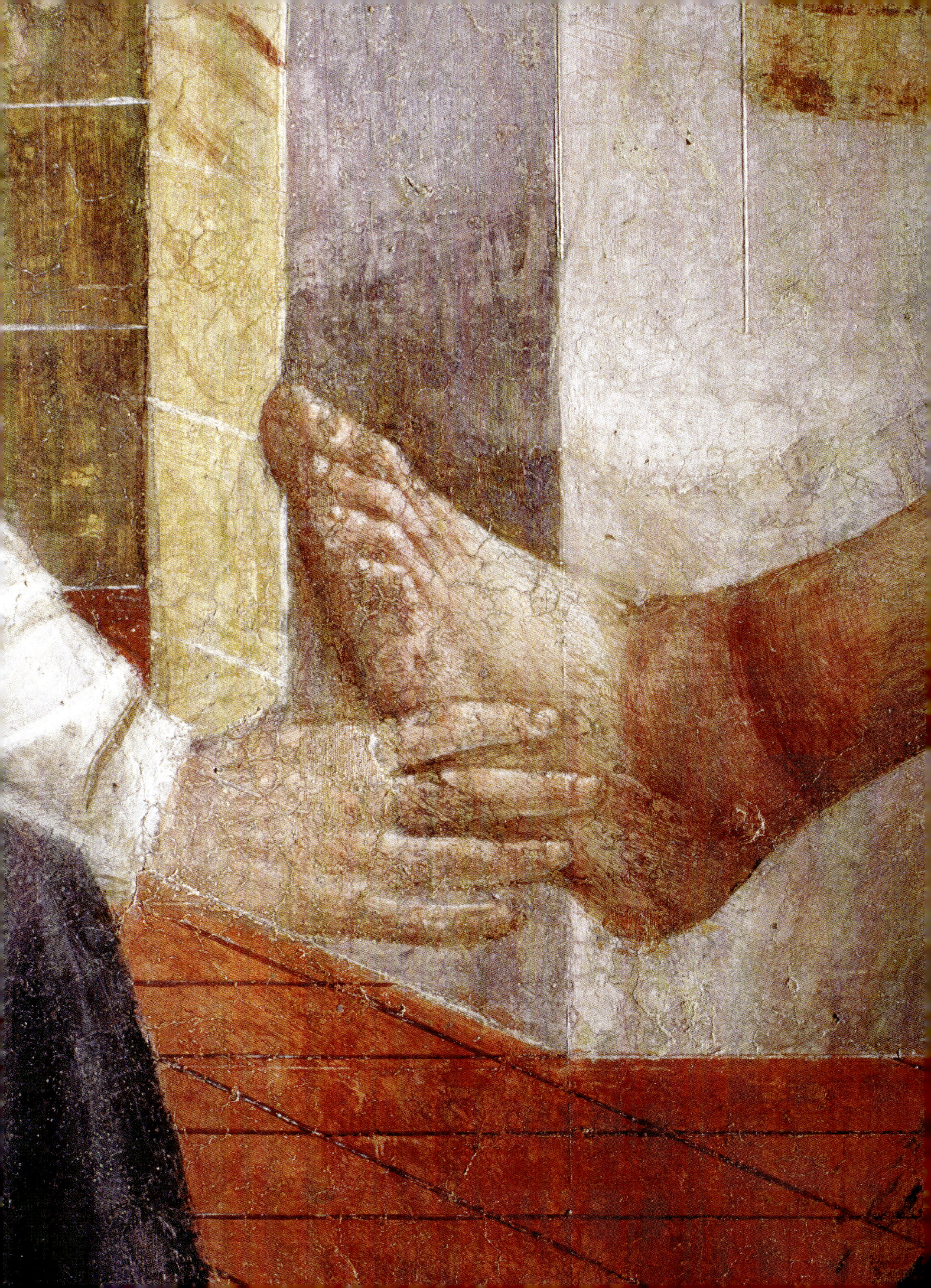

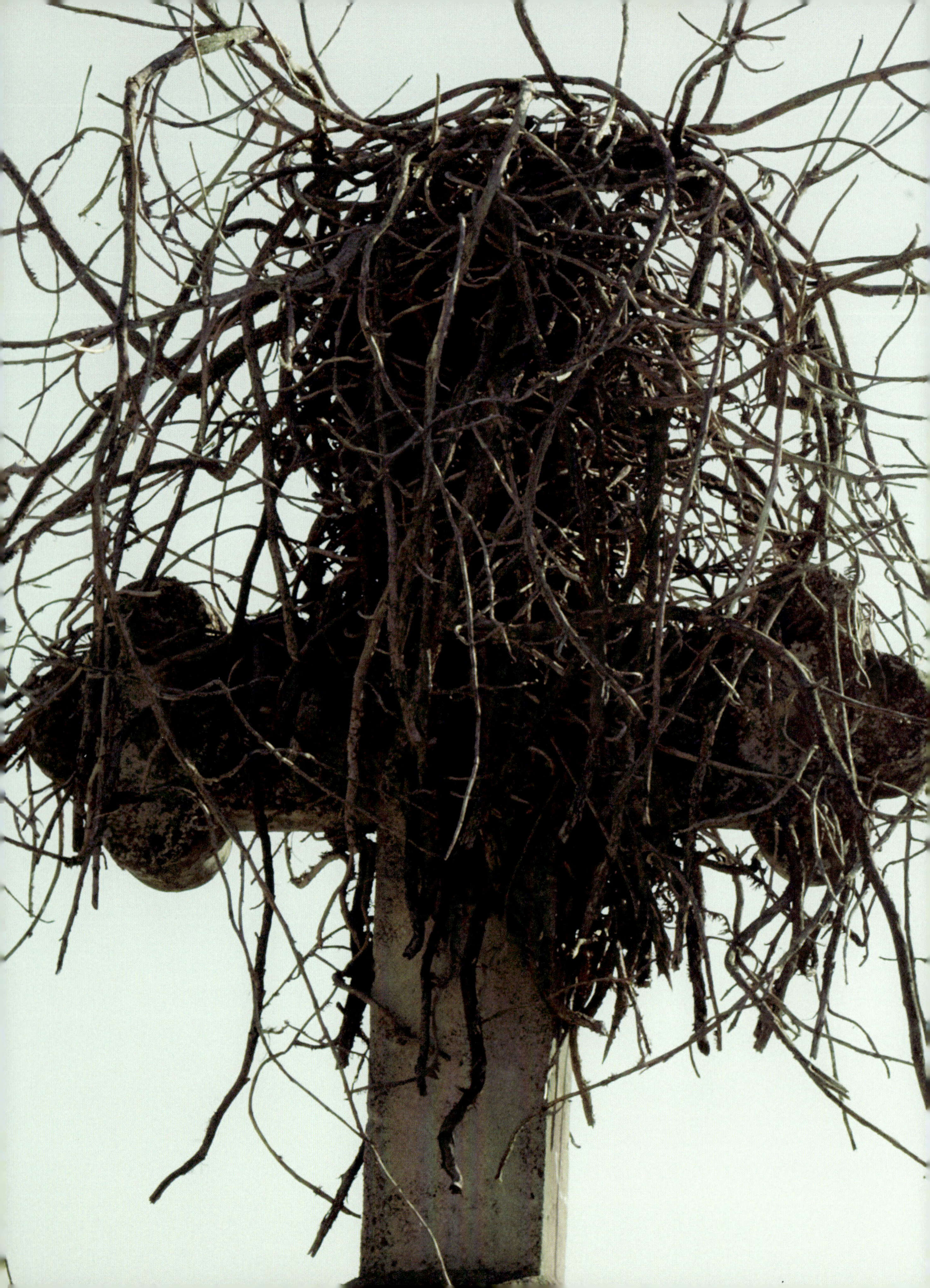

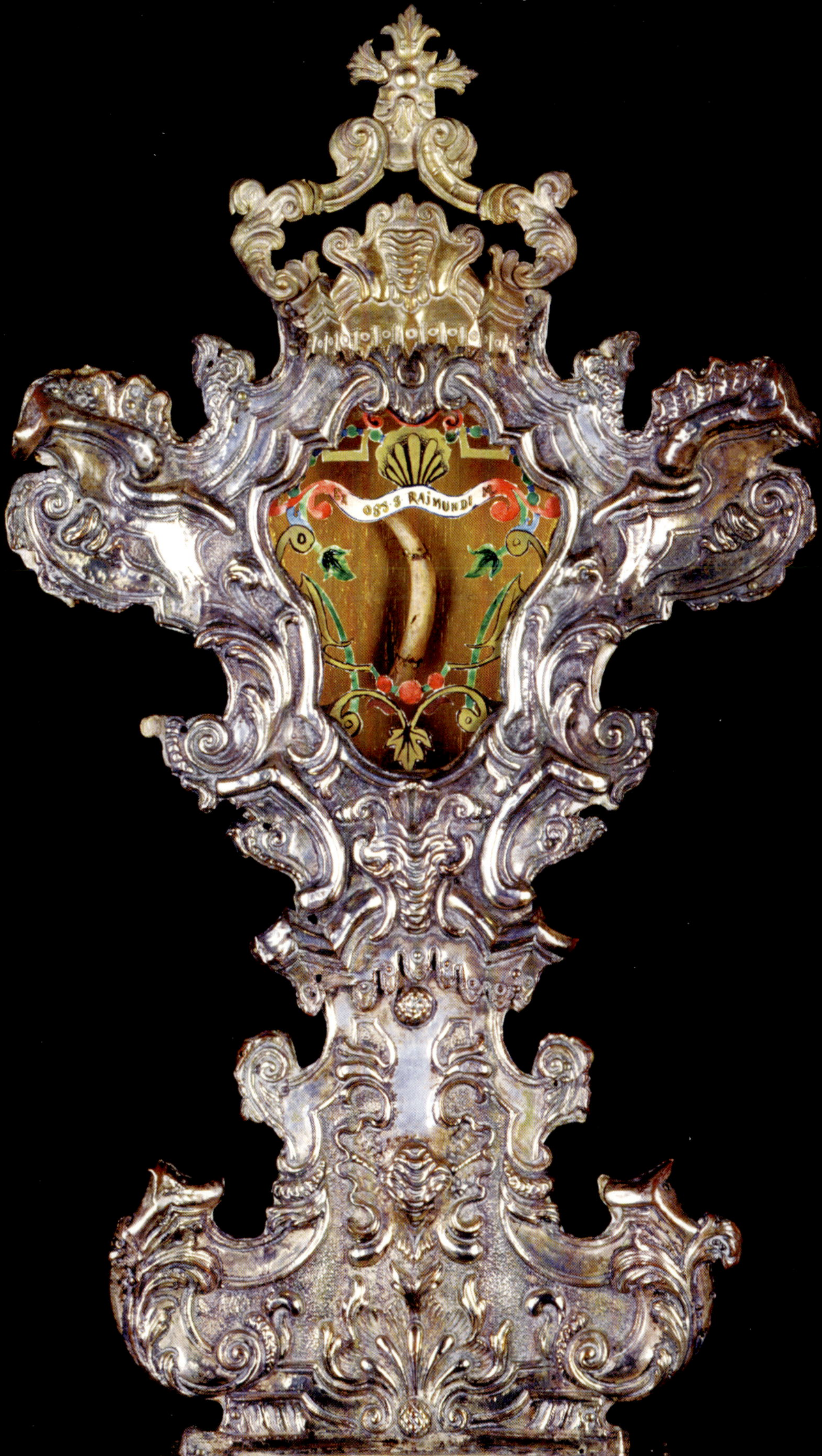
OSS · S RAJMUNDI

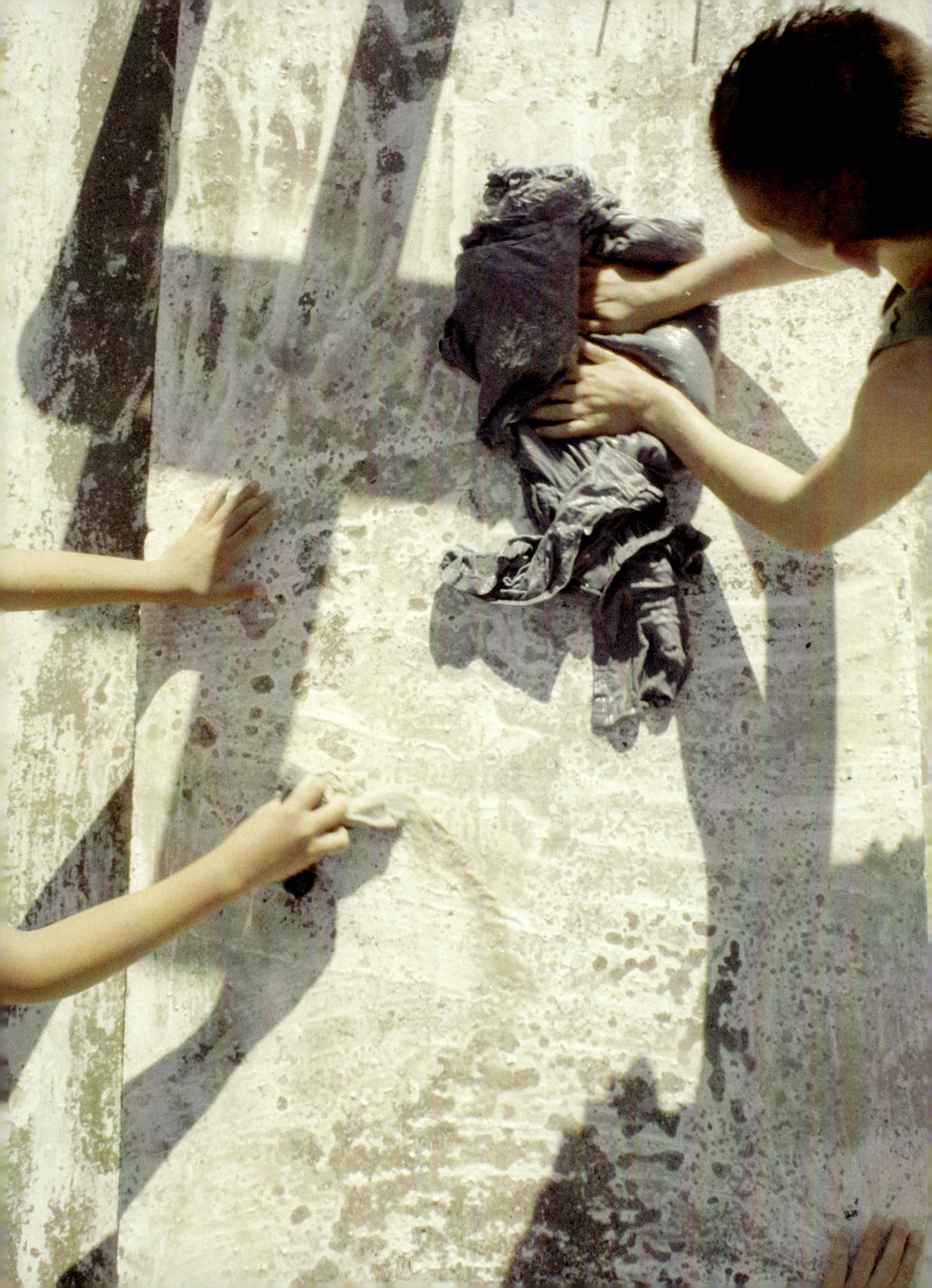

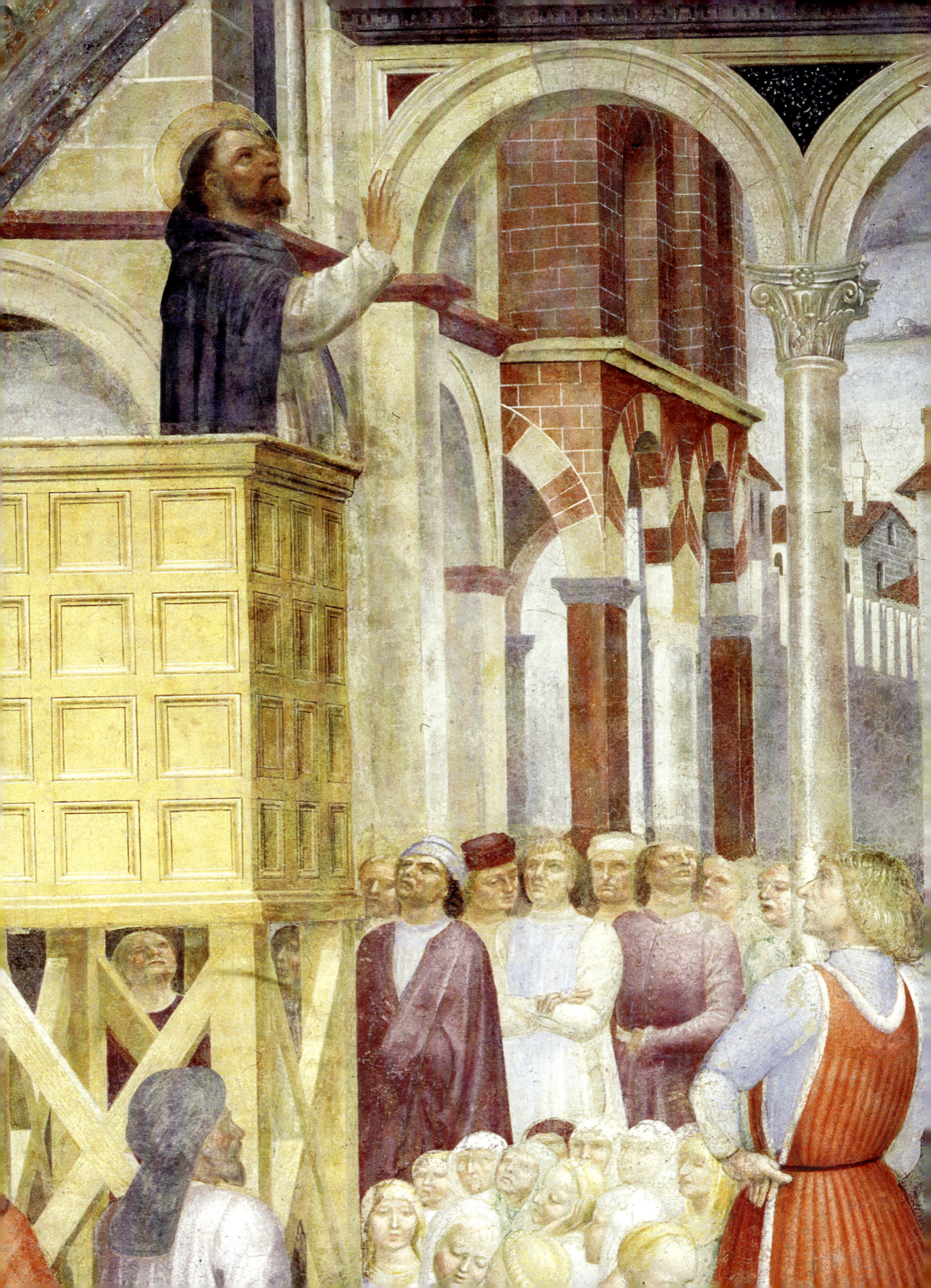

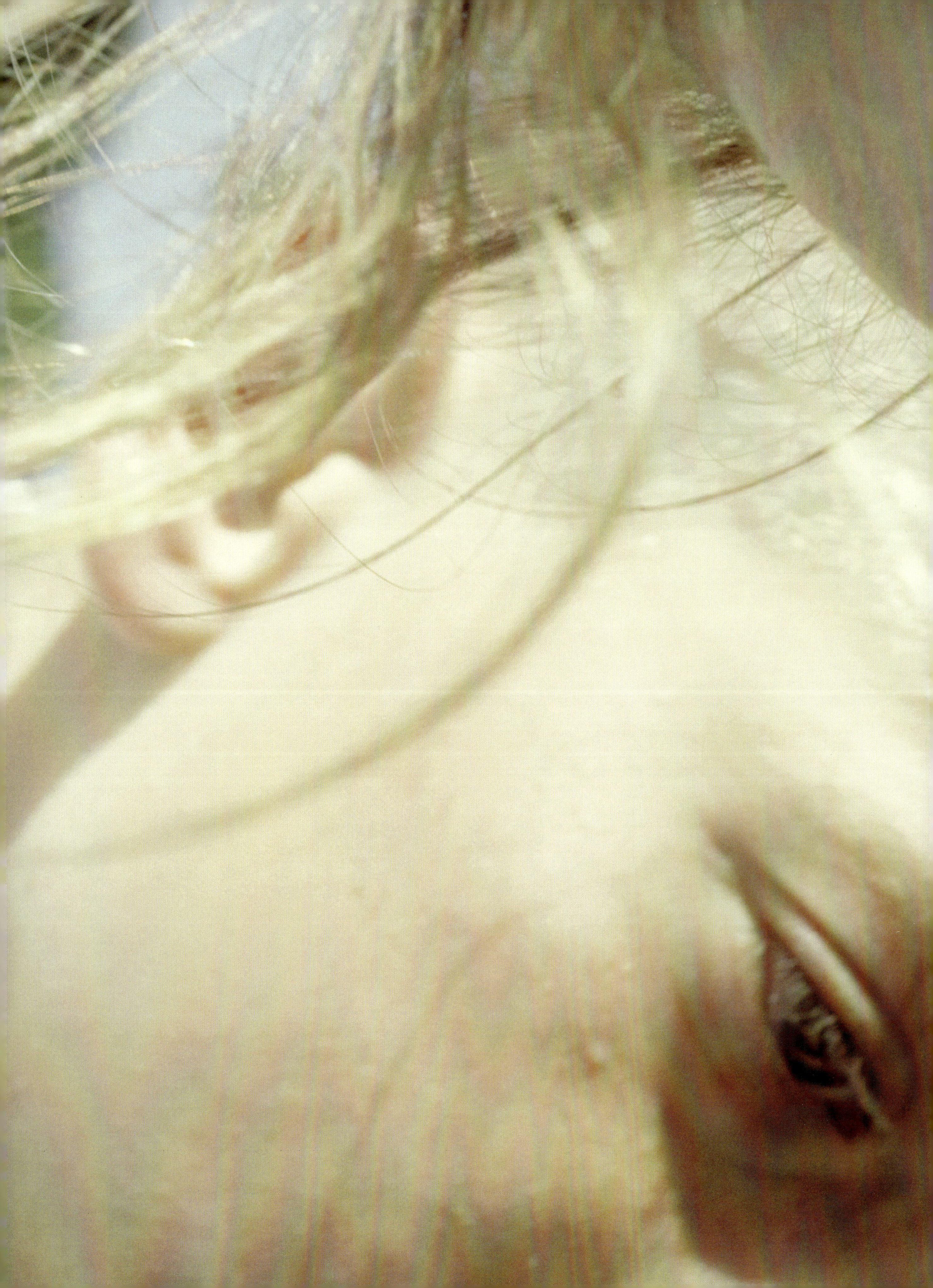

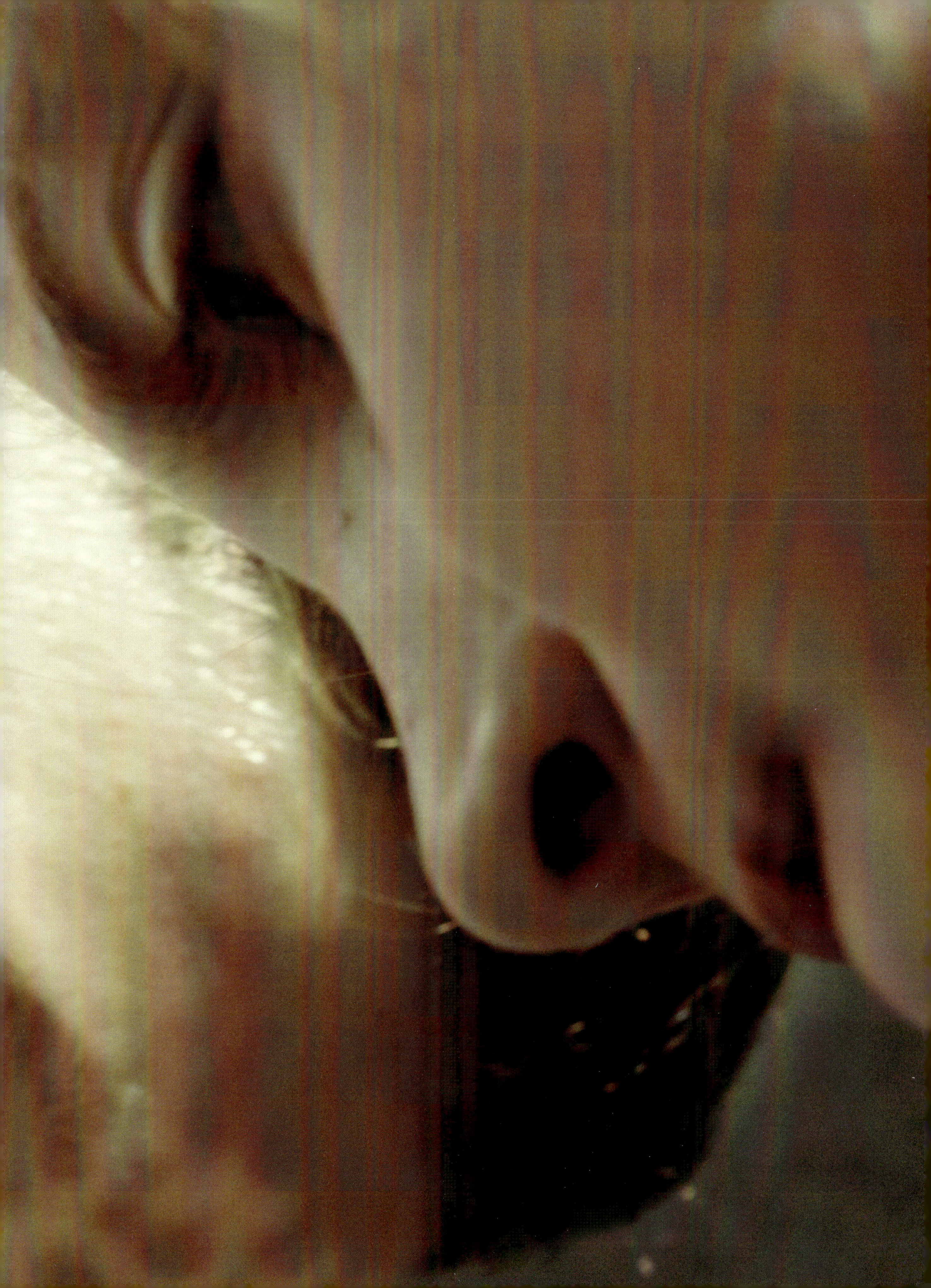

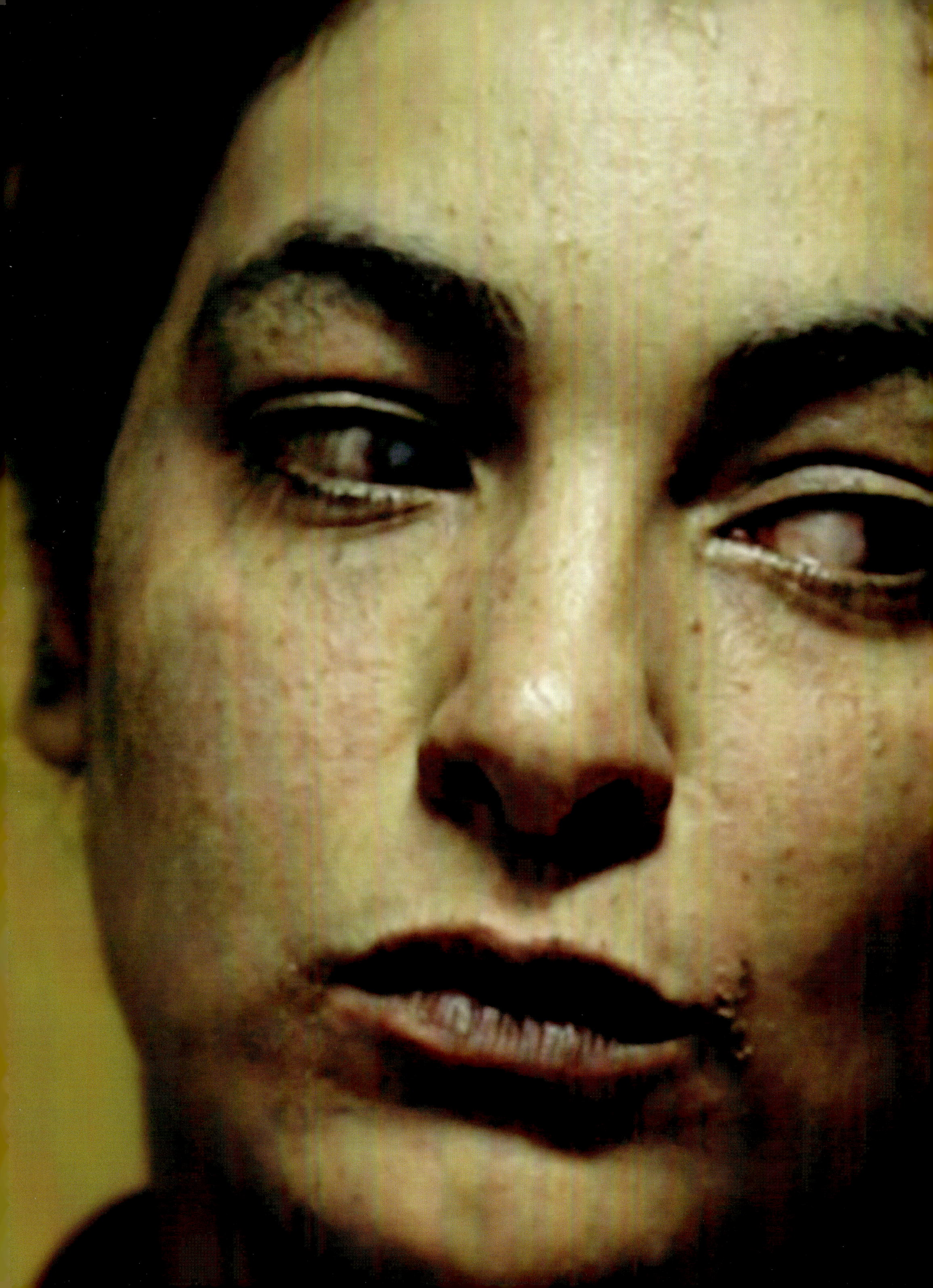

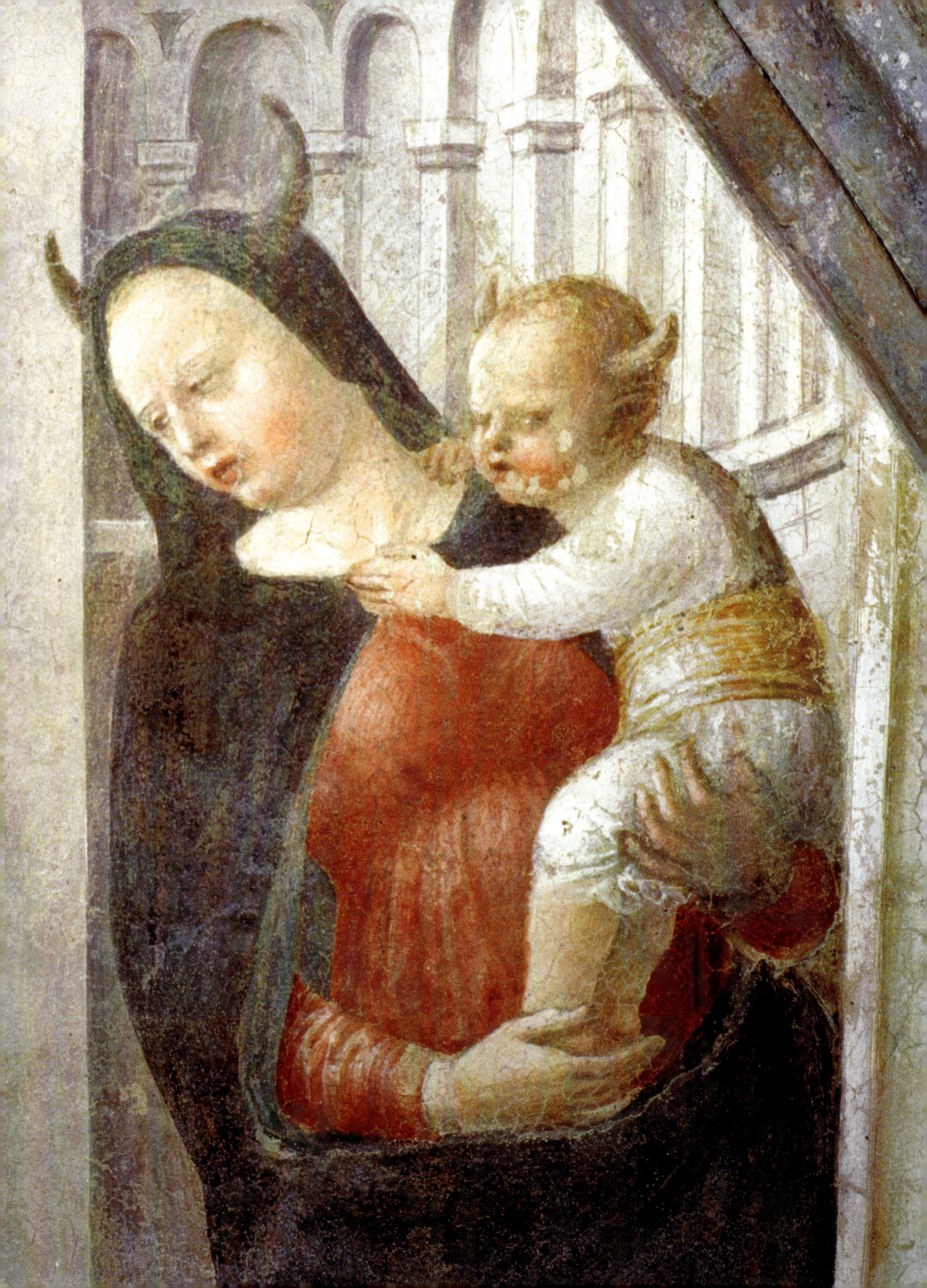

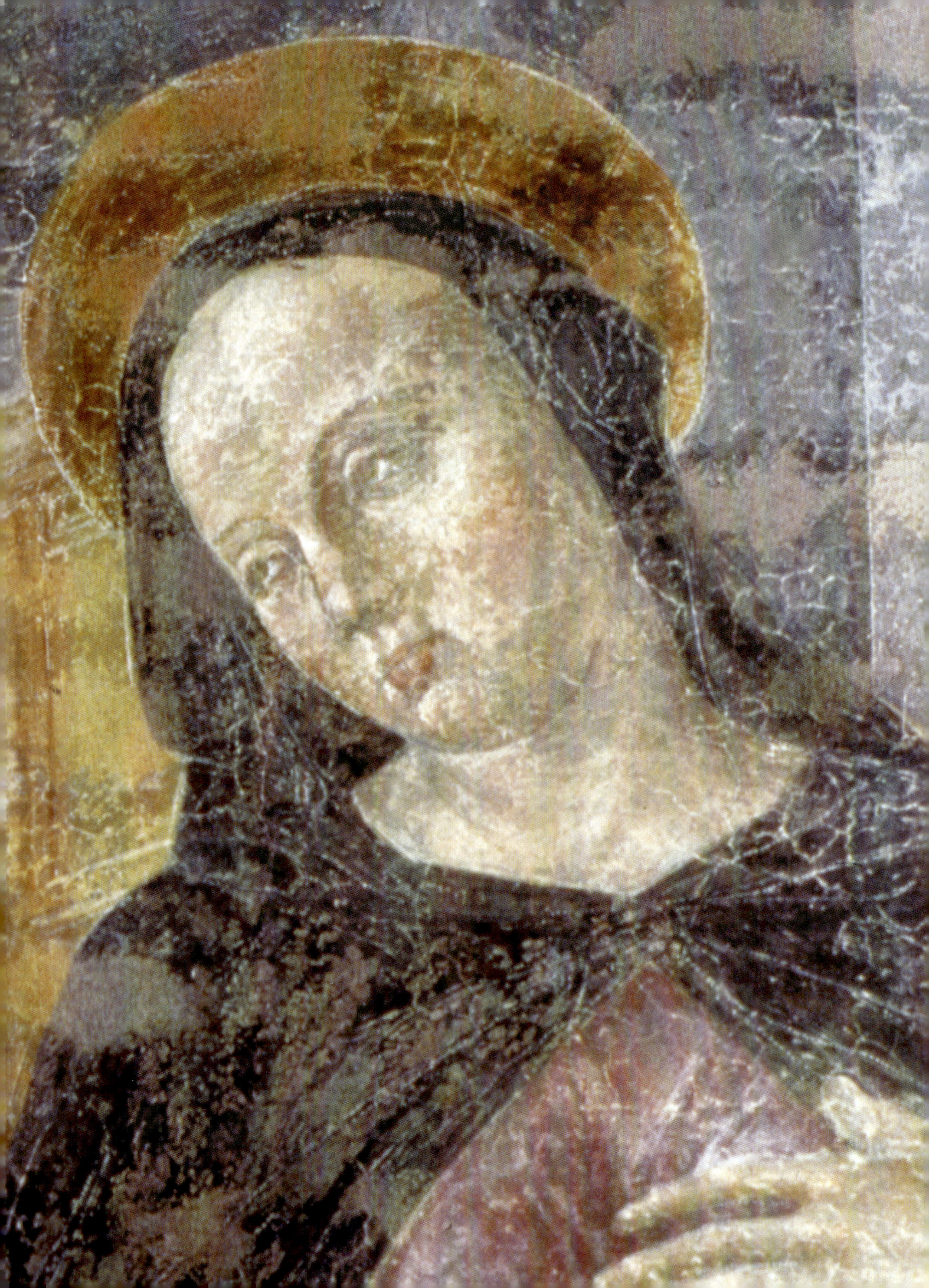

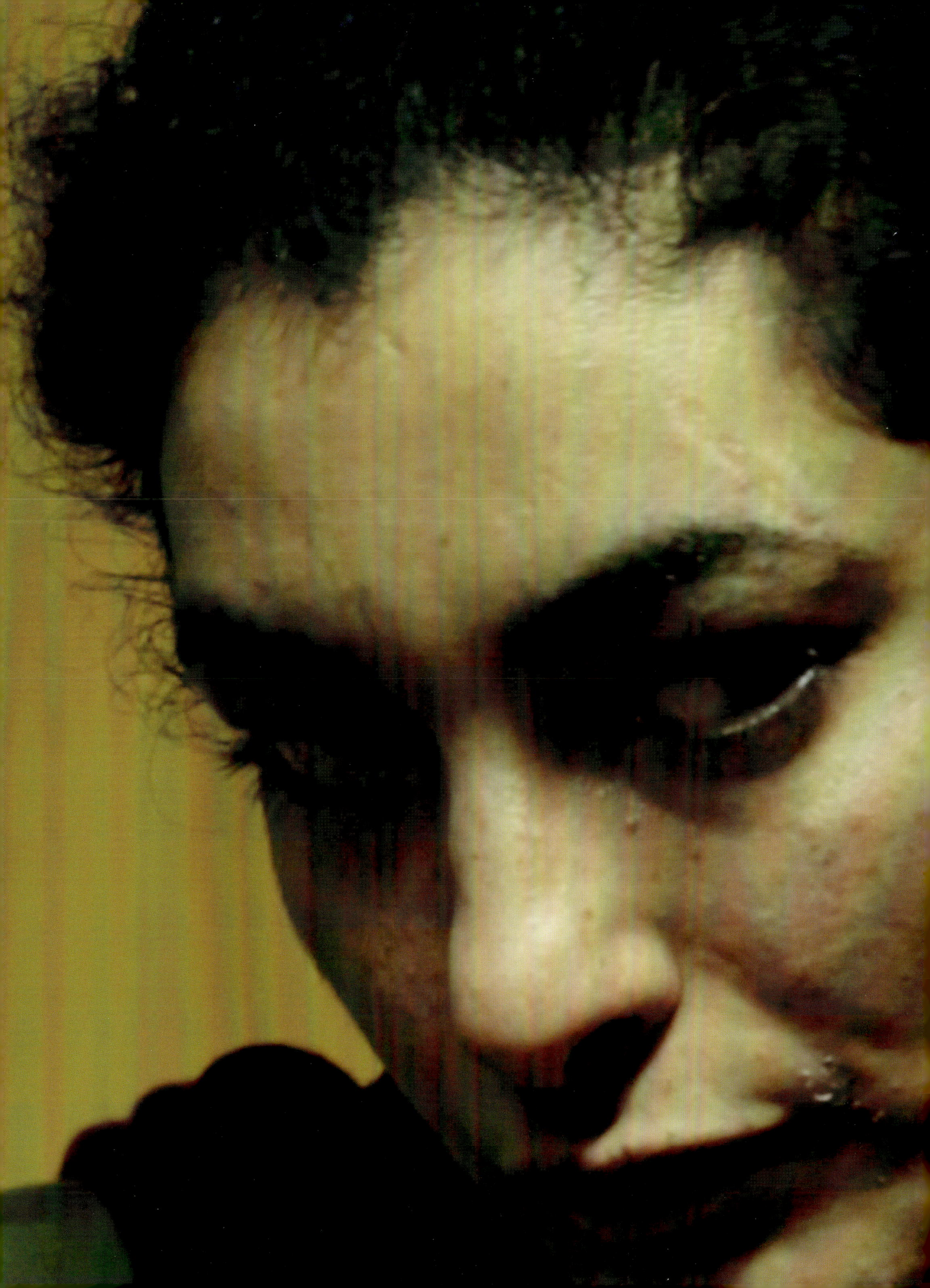

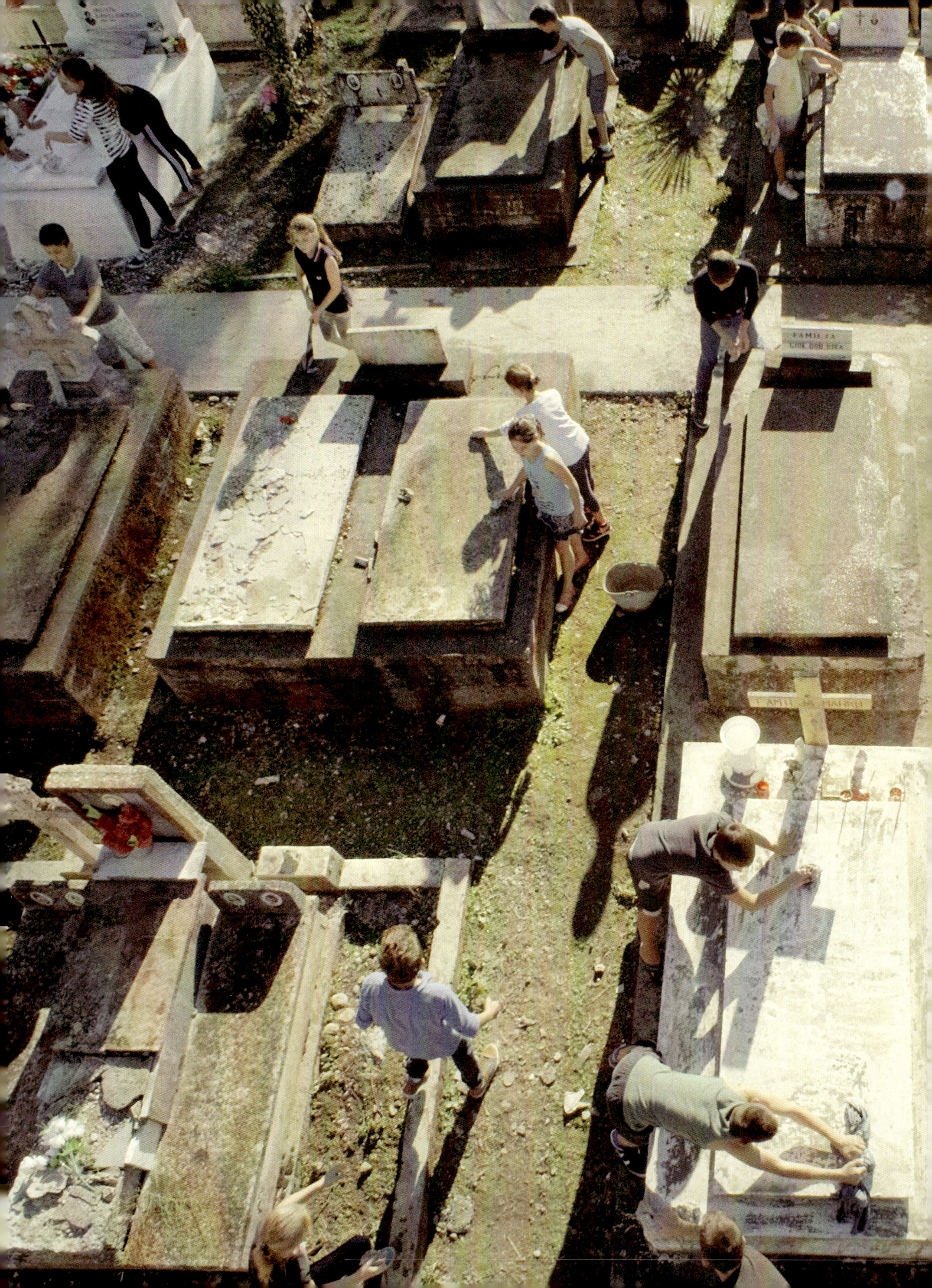

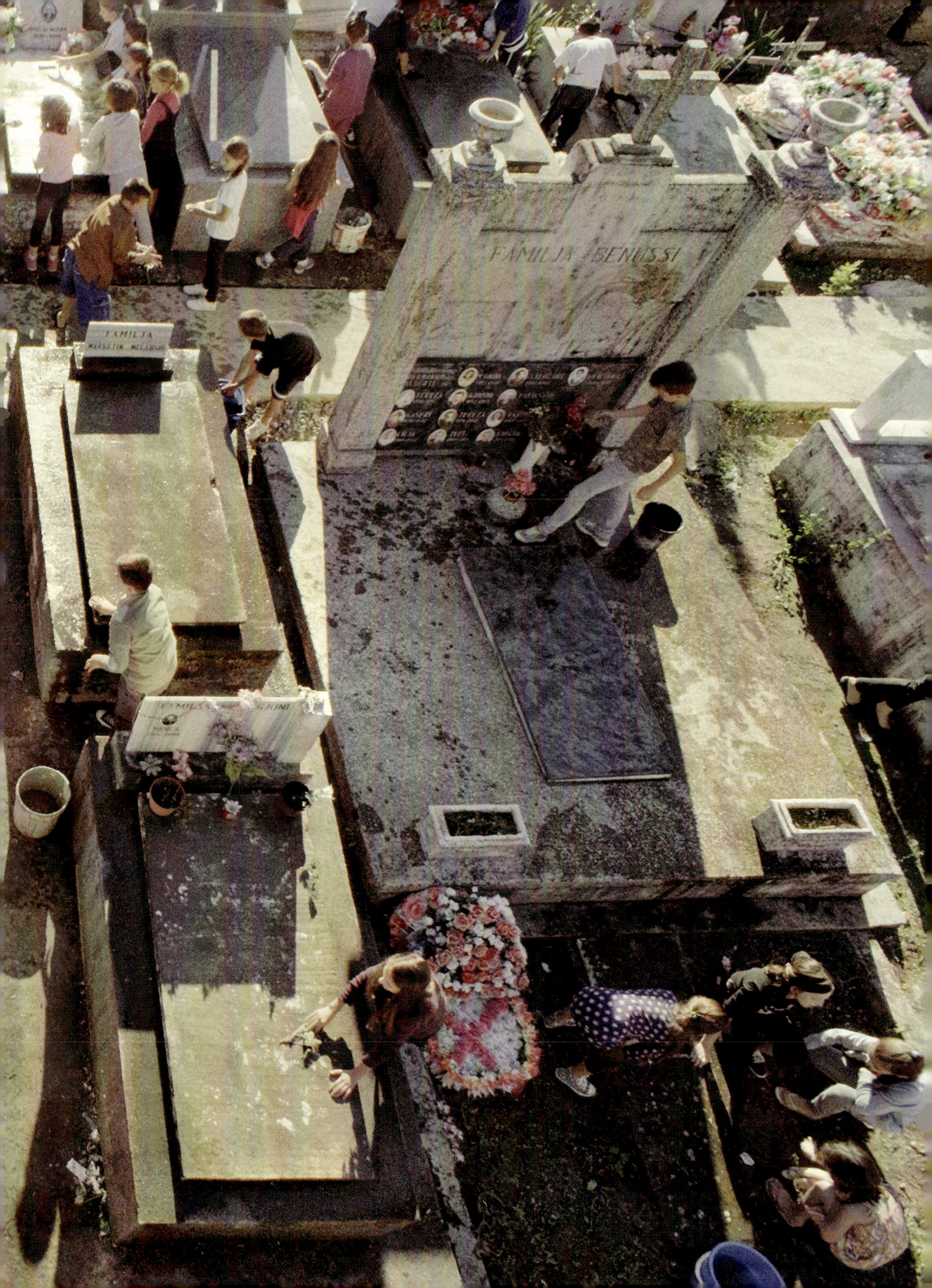
FAMILJA BENUSSI
FAMILJA

The book is published on the occasion of the exhibition /
Il libro è stato pubblicato in occasione della mostra

Adrian Paci
The Guardians

Chiostri di Sant'Eustorgio, Milano
March 28th–October 1st 2017
28 marzo–01 ottobre 2017

Curated by / A cura di
Gabi Scardi

Produced by / Prodotta da
Chiostri di Sant'Eustorgio, Milano

with the support of / con il sostegno di
kaufmann repetto, Milano / New York
Peter Kilchmann, Zurich

CHIOSTRI DI SANT'EUSTORGIO kaufmann repetto Galerie Peter Kilchmann

Publisher / Editore
Mousse Publishing, Milano
moussepublishing.com

Edited by / A cura di
Gabi Scardi

Publishing Editor
Ilaria Bombelli

Design
Mousse

Texts / Testi
Charles Esche, Gabi Scardi

Translations / Traduzioni
Teresa Albanese, Johanna Bishop

Editing / Correzione bozze
Lindsey Westbrook

Printed by / Stampato da
Artigiana Grafica

Photo credits / Crediti fotografici
Andrea Rossetti

© 2017 Mousse Publishing; kaufmann repetto, Milano / New York; Peter Kilchmann, Zurich;
the artist, the authors of the texts, the photographer / l'artista, gli autori dei testi, il fotografo

All rights reserved in all countries, including translation, total or partial adaptation and reproduction by any means (including microfilm, film and photocopies), as well as electronic storage / La traduzione, l'adattamento totale o parziale, la riproduzione con qualsiasi mezzo (compresi i microfilm, i film, le fotocopie), nonché la memorizzazione elettronica, sono riservati per tutti i paesi.

The publisher would like to thank the Chiostri di Sant'Eustorgio museum staff and all those who have kindly given their permission for the reproduction of material for this book. Every effort has been made to obtain permission to reproduce the images and texts in this catalogue. However, as is standard editorial policy, the publisher is at the disposal of copyright holders and undertakes to correct any omissions or errors in future editions / L'editore ringrazia sentitamente il personale del museo dei Chiostri di Sant'Eustorgio e tutti coloro che hanno concesso le fotografie e i diritti di riproduzione su testi e immagini, e resta a disposizione di tutti i proprietari di diritti sulle immagini nel caso non si fosse riusciti a reperirli per chiedere debita autorizzazione.

Printed in Italy / Stampato in Italia

ISBN 978-88-6749-301-2
20 EUR